Lake
Saimaa

Kymi River

GULF OF FINLAND

Kokemäki River

GULF OF

ALAND
ISLANDS

GOTLAND

BALTIC SEA

OLAND

Dal River

Lake
Mälar

Lake
Silja

Lake
Hjälmar

Lake
Vätter

BORNHOLM

Lake
Väner

SMALAND

Glomma River

ORESUND

Lagen River

Oslo Fjord

KATTEGAT

ZEALAND

GREAT BELT

JOSTEDALSBRE

SKAGERRAK

THE SKAW

Sogne Fjord

Hardanger Fjord

JUTLAND

SCANDINAVIA

DENMARK

ICELAND

NORWAY

FINLAND

SWEDEN

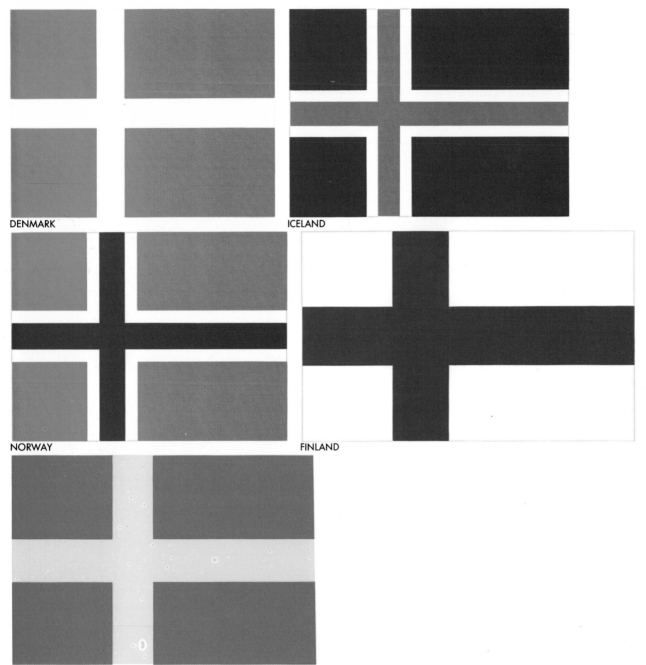

DENMARK

ICELAND

NORWAY

FINLAND

SWEDEN

SCANDINAVIA

By the Editors of Time-Life Books

TIME-LIFE BOOKS ○ ALEXANDRIA, VIRGINIA

Time-Life Books Inc.
is a wholly owned subsidiary of

TIME INCORPORATED

FOUNDER: Henry R. Luce 1898-1967

Editor-in-Chief: Henry Anatole Grunwald
Chairman and Chief Executive Officer: J. Richard Munro
President and Chief Operating Officer: N. J. Nicholas Jr.
Chairman of the Executive Committee: Ralph P. Davidson
Corporate Editor: Ray Cave
Group Vice President, Books: Reginald K. Brack Jr.
Vice President, Books: George Artandi

TIME-LIFE BOOKS INC.

EUROPEAN EDITOR: Kit van Tulleken
Assistant European Editor: Gillian Moore
Design Director: Ed Skyner
Photography Director: Pamela Marke
Chief of Research: Vanessa Kramer
Chief Sub-editor: Ilse Gray

LIBRARY OF NATIONS

Series Editor: Tony Allan

Editorial Staff for *Scandinavia*
Editor: John Cottrell
Deputy Editor: Ellen Galford
Researcher: Susan Dawson
Designer: Mary Staples
Sub-editor: Sally Rowland
Picture Department: Christine Hinze, Peggy Tout
Editorial Assistant: Molly Oates

EDITORIAL PRODUCTION

Chief: Jane Hawker
Production Assistants: Alan Godwin, Maureen Kelly
Editorial Department: Theresa John, Debra Lelliott,
Sylvia Osborne

Special Contributors: The chapter texts were written by
Windsor Chorlton, Michael Frenchman, Frederic V.
Grunfeld, W. R. Mead and Barry Turner
Other Contributors: Patricia Clough and Hazel Evans

Assistant Editor for the U.S. Edition: Barbara
Fairchild Quarmby

CONSULTANT

W. R. Mead is Professor Emeritus of Geography at University College, London. He
has written several books on Scandinavia,
among them *An Historical Geography of
Scandinavia* and *An Economic Geography of
the Scandinavian Countries and Finland.*

Library of Congress Cataloguing in Publication Data
Scandinavia.
    (Library of nations; 13)
    Bibliography: p.
    Includes index.
    Summary: An introduction to the geography,
history, economy, government, and people of
Denmark, Norway, Sweden, Iceland, and Finland.
    1. Scandinavia. 2. Finland. [1. Scandinavia.
2. Finland] I. Time-Life Books. II. Series: Library
of nations (Alexandria, Va.); 13.
DL5.S37 1987   948   86-30132
ISBN 0-8094-5177-8
ISBN 0-8094-5178-6 (lib. bdg.)

Cover: Three pedestrians, warmly clad
against the winter cold, make their way
past the modern Tromsdalen Church in
Tromso, northern Norway. Built of
concrete and glass, the structure is
known as the Cathedral of the Arctic.

Front and back endpapers: A topographic
map showing the major rivers, lakes,
mountain ranges and other natural
features of Scandinavia appears on the
front endpaper. The back endpaper
shows the five countries of Scandinavia,
with the principal towns and islands.

CONTENTS

A glowing sun, still hovering above the horizon at 1 o'clock in the morning, casts an eerie light over Reisa Fjord in northern Norway. The "Midnight Sun,"

6

SCANDINAVIA'S WIDE OPEN SPACES

Most of Scandinavia's land area, which totals 485,475 square miles — slightly larger than Alaska — is taken up by Sweden, Finland and Norway, respectively the fourth, fifth and sixth biggest states in Europe. Large areas of each country are sparsely inhabited, however, so population density figures are generally low — a characteristic most evident in Iceland, which averages six people per square mile. (Montana averages about 5.5 people per square mile.) Only smaller, intensively cultivated Denmark has a density approaching the crowded Western European norm.

	ICELAND	NORWAY	FINLAND	DENMARK	SWEDEN	
	240,443	4,145,845	4,784,710	5,111,108	8,342,621	Population
	6	33	38	308	48	Population density (people per sq. mile)
	39,769	125,052	130,559	16,633	173,732	Area (in sq. miles)
	Reykjavik	Oslo	Helsinki	Copenhagen	Stockholm	Capital

visible in midsummer only in districts north of the Arctic Circle, is one of the strangest and most distinctive features of the Scandinavian world.

WINTERS TEMPERED BY THE SEA

	°C	°F
	0 to 4	32 to 40
	-4 to 0	25 to 32
	-8 to -4	18 to 25
	-12 to -8	10 to 18
	-16 to -12	3 to 10

	°C	°F
Moscow	-9.9	14.2
Helsinki	-5.4	22.3
Oslo	-4.7	23.5
Stockholm	-2.9	26.8
Berlin	-0.5	31.1
Reykjavik	-0.4	31.3
Copenhagen	0.1	32.2
New York	0.9	33.6
Tokyo	3.7	38.7
London	4.2	39.6

In spite of its northerly location, much of Scandinavia experiences relatively mild winters, as shown in the chart on the left, which compares January mean temperatures in various northern cities. In the west, this mildness is caused by the relatively warm currents of the North Atlantic Drift and accompanying westerly winds, which keep the tidal salt waters around Iceland, Denmark, Norway and southwest Sweden free of ice. To the east, however, high-pressure systems forming over Eastern Europe cause the brackish waters of the Gulfs of Bothnia and Finland to freeze over. As a result, the north of Sweden and Finland are the coldest parts of the area in winter.

Warmly wrapped against the snow, a woman basks in the sun beside an annex to

her wooden vacation cabin in Mörkedalen, a valley in southern Norway popular with skiers during the longer, late-winter days of March and April.

Sea birds flock around a trawler off the Westman Islands, south of Iceland. Although fishermen account for only 5 percent of Iceland's work force, their

catch provides the raw material for about 75 percent of all exports, in the form of fish-derived meal and oils, as well as fresh and preserved fish.

A UNIVERSALLY HIGH STANDARD OF LIVING

Thriving economies and an egalitarian spread of wealth — the income of a Swedish Cabinet minister in 1984 was about double that of a factory worker — have ensured a high standard of living for most Scandinavians. Figures for gross national product per capita are among the highest in the world. Sweden, once second only to Switzerland internationally, was overtaken in the early 1980s by Norway, as the latter began to benefit from the exploitation of its North Sea oil and gas fields. Denmark at that time stood fifth and Finland 11th in personal income.

Universal affluence has meant that ownership of expensive consumer goods, such as color TVs, refrigerators, freezers and cars, is the norm for most Scandinavian families. Second homes, too, are increasingly common. Norwegians, for example, owned 300,000 vacation homes in 1984 — one for every five households — as well as 250,000 pleasure boats. Nor is public spending neglected: A large proportion of personal income is diverted through taxation to finance social services that are among the most comprehensive in the world.

On an island in the Stockholm archipelago, two young women relax outside a vacation house. Behind them stands a sauna with a stockpile of wood stored

underneath. The thousands of small islands that dot the Baltic to the east of the Swedish capital are popular locations for city dwellers' second homes.

Water from the Lagen River, swollen by rain, pours through the floodgates of the Hunderfossen Dam, a hydroelectric power plant near Lillehammer in

POWER FROM THE RIVERS

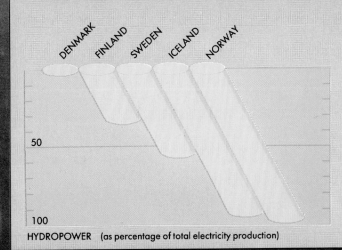

DENMARK FINLAND SWEDEN ICELAND NORWAY

50

100

HYDROPOWER (as percentage of total electricity production)

Water is the most important resource for generating electricity in Norway, Iceland and Sweden, where fast-flowing rivers have encouraged the building of hydroelectric power stations. In Norway, indeed, hydropower meets 99.8 percent of electricity demand, and the figure is almost as high in Iceland, even though only about 10 percent of the country's available water resources are exploited. Most of Sweden's hydroelectric potential is already developed; to meet extra demand, the nation currently depends chiefly on nuclear energy. Finland also gets much of its energy supply from nuclear reactors, while Denmark relies almost entirely on imported coal and oil for electric power.

southern Norway. Most of the nation's hydropower projects are located in the south, where rainfall is heaviest.

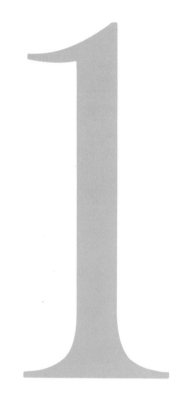

A UNION OF NATIONS

Encircled by sea and hills, the port of Alesund on the rugged west coast of Norway is one of many Scandinavian settlements that are intricately bound to waterside settings. The majority of Nordic people live close to the sea or along rivers or lakes.

In the first century A.D., when writing his monumental *Historia Naturalis,* Roman encyclopedist Pliny the Elder made the first-known reference to Scandinavia. Beyond indicating that it lay in northwestern Europe, he failed to define the region clearly; and now, nearly 2,000 years later, there is still confusion and disagreement about Scandinavia's true definitions. Some geographers argue that it is purely and simply the huge mountainous peninsula shared by Norway and Sweden. Traditionalists tend to see it as a trio of ancient kingdoms — Denmark, Norway and Sweden — which were once united under a single crown. More usually, however, the name is applied abroad to Denmark, Finland, Iceland, Norway and Sweden — five nations linked by religious, historical and geographical ties, and now bound together more closely than any other group of politically independent countries.

The functional integration within the frontiers of Scandinavia is unique in the world. Under the terms of the 1962 Helsinki Treaty, these five Nordic states — who prefer the term "Norden" to describe their collective presence — undertake to maintain and develop cooperation in legal, cultural, social and economic fields. They have a common postage rate and increasingly harmonized industrial, commercial, legal and educational systems. They constitute a common labor market and a common passport area: They are integrated to such a degree that Danes, Finns, Icelanders, Norwegians and Swedes enjoy a remarkable degree of mutual citizenship, and they have almost as much freedom of movement and settlement as Americans have within the 50 states of the United States.

The extent of this Scandinavian cooperation was dramatically illustrated on September 3, 1967. On that day, the so-called H-day — H for *hoger,* meaning "right" — Sweden made the switch to driving on the right-hand side of the road to conform with the neighboring Nordic partners. For more than two centuries, left-side traffic had been the official practice in Sweden. But in 1963 the government decided to make a change, even though it involved years of preparation at a cost of 600 million kronor (then almost $120 million). The following year, Iceland also switched to the right, so completing Nordic harmony in traffic procedures.

Ostensibly, such a degree of Nordic conformity is extraordinary when one considers that Scandinavia's 22.5 million inhabitants are scattered far and wide over lands variously separated by the Baltic Sea, the North Sea and the Atlantic Ocean. Iceland, the most isolated country in Europe, lies some 560 miles from the peninsula of Norway and Sweden. Excluding the icy wastes of Greenland, which is officially a constituent part of Denmark although it is now self-governing, Scandinavia has a land area of 485,475 square miles —

greater than the countries of Britain, France and West Germany combined.

On the other hand, geography contributes in many ways to the sense of community felt by the Nordic countries. All are high-latitude lands on the northwest fringe of Europe. All of them suffer high costs in maintaining their communications systems because of the nature of their topography and, Denmark excepted, because of the severity of their winters. All five countries possess a limited variety of natural resources, though some of these resources — for example, timber in Finland and Sweden — are abundant. All have relatively small populations and, again with the exception of Denmark, have large tracts of wilderness.

Historically, the five Nordic countries were first united in 1397 when Queen Margrete of Denmark established the Union of Kalmar, joining Denmark, Norway and Sweden, along with the dependencies of Iceland and Finland, under one crown. The union

formally ended with the secession of Sweden in 1523. However, Norway and Denmark (then including Iceland and the Faeroe Islands) remained united for several centuries under a single monarchy; and Finland had six and a half centuries of close association with Sweden before being ceded to Russia in 1809 and becoming a grand duchy.

In social terms, too, the Nordic countries have developed many common characteristics. The five countries are now urbanized, and Iceland apart, they have modern industrial and service economies. All have egalitarian societies, comprehensive social security systems and very high standards of living. Denmark, Norway and Sweden are constitutional monarchies, whereas

Iceland and Finland have elected presidents as their heads of state. The difference, however, is only cosmetic. Fundamentally, all the countries are Western-style parliamentary democracies that are governed by proportional

representation; and all have so many well-supported political parties that coalition governments prevail.

Scandinavians are also linked by the Lutheran religion — to which 95 percent of the population of the five countries nominally adheres — and by the close linguistic ties of the Danes, Swedes, Icelanders and Norwegians. Finnish belongs to a totally different language group. However, Finland is officially bilingual, and most Finns

The faces of a random collection of Scandinavians — from a Norwegian woman to an elderly, bearded Lapland-er — reveal that, despite the blond, blue-eyed Nordic stereotype, the northern lands are home to a diversity of peoples and physiognomies.

have some understanding of their second language, Swedish, which is a compulsory subject in high school. Moreover, when Scandinavians are unable to communicate in one of their own languages, they rely on English — taught to virtually all schoolchildren — to bridge the gap.

Scandinavian unity on a significant scale dates from 1952, with the establishment of the Nordic Council, an organization set up by Norway, Sweden,

Denmark and Iceland for cooperation between their governments. Finland became a member in 1955. More recently, Denmark's Atlantic outposts, Greenland and the Faeroe Islands, together with the Aland Islands (an autonomous province of Finland in the Baltic) have been granted the right to nominate their own representatives.

The first significant achievements of the Nordic Council came in 1954 when the member countries agreed to a common labor market, which enabled their nationals to work and settle in any of the signatory lands without a work permit or a permanent resident's visa. Since then, more than one million people have migrated from one Nordic country to another, the greatest flow being from Finland into Sweden.

Additional examples of Nordic cooperation include collaboration in the use of transatlantic satellite links in the exchange and production of television programs, in tackling environmental

problems, in constructing international highways and bridges, in jointly awarding prizes for the arts and in making grants for translating literary works from one Scandinavian language into another. An international airline company, the Scandinavian Airlines System, or SAS, is operated by public and private capital from Denmark, Norway and Sweden. The power systems of Denmark, Finland, Norway and Sweden are interconnected so that surpluses of electricity can be transferred across their borders. There is also close cooperation between labor unions, sports and youth associations, and Nordic societies — groups working in each country to promote better understanding among Scandinavian states.

In addition, the Nordic countries coordinate regional planning in certain border areas where they may share services such as municipal fire brigades, schools and hospitals, and they work together in respect of their common interests such as tourism, road construc-

1

tion and communications. No part of Scandinavia stands to benefit more from this arrangement than those provinces of Finland, Norway and Sweden that are situated partly or entirely within the Arctic Circle. In this region — known as Nordkalotten because its cartographic shape resembles the calotte, or skullcap, worn by a priest — some 930,000 inhabitants are widely scattered over a mostly barren area of almost 118,000 square miles, and very often far removed from centers of supply and demand.

The other main area of coordinated planning in Scandinavia is the Oresund: a Danish-Swedish metropolitan region with a population of 2.8 million, which embraces both sides of the Sound, the narrow channel of water that separates Denmark and southwest Sweden. In 1964, a Dano-Swedish Oresund Council was established to consider matters of mutual interest, including pollution problems and joint development of cultural and leisure amenities. Plans for integrating the Oresund conurbation include the construction of a bridge over the Sound, connecting the Copenhagen area and the southwest coast of Sweden.

Over the years, this unusually close family of five nations has suffered its share of shocks and setbacks, most conspicuously in respect to trading agreements. In 1947, a Scandinavian customs union was proposed and then rejected. In 1970, a Danish initiative for a Scandinavian common market was turned down by the Finns because of their economic links with the Soviet Union. Three years later, Denmark joined the European Common Market (EEC) and Finland signed trade treaties with Comecon, the council for mutual economic assistance among socialist

countries that was founded in 1949.

However, despite this divergence, the Nordic countries continue to have strong common trade interests, especially by way of the European Free Trade Association (EFTA), founded in 1959. Denmark, Norway, Sweden and Iceland are members of EFTA, and Finland has been an associate member since 1961. This trading alliance has been a key factor in the increase of intra-Nordic trade, which has grown twice as fast as Nordic foreign trade. To a lesser degree, the EEC also represents a trading link; only Denmark is a member, but all the other Nordic countries have concluded bilateral agreements with the community.

There is less uniformity in the crucial area of defense. In 1948, Sweden proposed the formation of a Scandinavian defense union that would have required the declared neutrality of all member countries, with a commitment to defend any member nation attacked by a third party. Denmark supported the proposal at first, but later came to share the view of Norway and Iceland (both of whom had proclaimed their neutrality in World War II with absolutely no effect) that such a union would offer them no real protection in the event of a major conflict. Meanwhile, Finland had signed a Treaty of Friendship, Cooperation and Mutual Assistance with the Soviet Union. This treaty leaves the defense of Finland to Finnish armed forces, but it allows for the possibility of military aid from either party if the other country is attacked by Germany, or countries that are allied with Germany.

Closer bonds between the countries are discouraged by the fact that, while the Nordic peoples have a strong sense of kinship, they also passionately cher-

ish their individualism and national independence. Throughout Scandinavia, national pride is evinced by the ubiquitous show of flags — on harbor fronts and at airports, on yachts and motorboats, at hotel entrances and on dinner tables, both public and private. Even the Faeroes and the Aland Islands have their own territorial flags. By contrast, there is no flag for Norden as a whole. Instead, at Nordic Council meetings, a flow of national flags flying side by side are seen as preferable to a single emblem.

Gylfi Gíslason, a former Icelandic Minister of Education and member of the Nordic Council, has explained: "Each nation has nurtured a strong patriotism that it is careful to preserve. Each considers the present collaboration no obstacle to these feelings; on the contrary, it is an encouragement. Thus it is no wonder that proposals for a Nordic state or union of states are invariably rejected, since no advantage that would accrue from such an alliance could be more important than the preservation of the culture and nationality of each individual state." Quite simply, although a remarkable degree of harmony exists, each Scandinavian state is a unique entity, steeped in its own mythologies, its inhabitants harboring emotions born of experiences particular to the terrains and territories of their homelands.

Of all the Scandinavian countries, Denmark is the most markedly different from the rest. It is by far the smallest — a mere 16,630 square miles, less than one fifth the size of the United Kingdom. It is the most low lying, its highest point being just 561 feet above sea level, and it has the mildest climate and the most amenable soils. Furthermore, it is

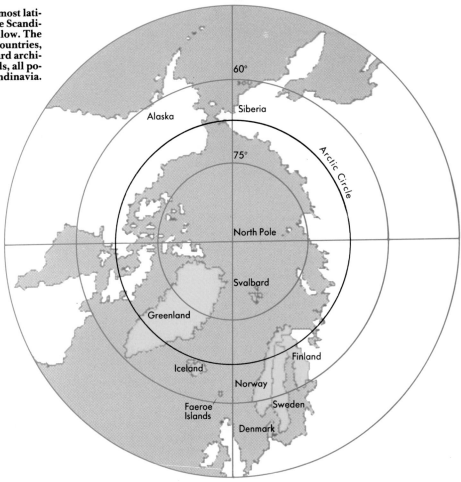

A global view of the northernmost latitudes reveals the extent of the Scandinavian world, here colored yellow. The map takes in the five Nordic countries, plus Greenland, the Svalbard archipelago and the Faeroe Islands, all politically part of Scandinavia.

the oldest inhabited part of Scandinavia (man is known to have lived there for at least 10,000 years); the most densely populated, with roughly 308 Danes to the square mile; and the most urban with more than 80 percent of its 5.1 million inhabitants living in cities or towns.

Denmark has a highly civilized landscape. Approximately 70 percent of its surface area is farmed, and another 10 percent is taken up by well-ordered woodland. It has heaths, bogs, dunes and salt marshes, but unlike the rest of Scandinavia, it is predominantly well tended and without any truly wild, untamed land. Nor, for that matter, is the country rich in natural resources beyond its farmland and coastal fisheries. The only basic raw materials are clay and chalk — the foundation of cement and brickmaking industries. In recent years, Denmark has gained a small share in the North Sea oil and natural-gas fields. Otherwise it is virtually devoid of mineral wealth.

The differences between Denmark and other Nordic countries extend to the people. The Danes tend to be more cosmopolitan in their attitudes and lifestyles. In part, this is explained by their country's location at major crossroads of international trade. The Danes live beside the North Sea's narrow gateway to the Baltic Sea, and their territory has always provided island steppingstones between central and northern Europe. As a result, its inhabitants have been subject to foreign intrusion, influence and intermarriage.

Denmark is a highly fragmented country. It is made up of the northern half of the peninsula of Jutland, together with 406 separate islands, of which Zealand and Funen are the largest. Ninety-seven islands are inhabited, and

no Dane lives more than 35 miles from the sea. The Danish capital Copenhagen is located on the east coast of Zealand, within sight of Skane, Sweden's southernmost province, which was once part of the kingdom of Denmark.

The West German federal state, or *Land,* of Schleswig-Holstein, constituting the southern part of the Jutland peninsula, was also formerly a part of the Danish realm. But now it is separated by a 42-mile-long border, Denmark's only land frontier. Northward, Danish Jutland trails away into a finger of land pointing toward Sweden, with its tip roughly on the same latitude as Gothenburg. The finger is called the Skaw, a great spit where picturesque lighthouses warn ships against treach-

erous sandbanks. At its northernmost point, tourists may be photographed with one foot in the North Sea and the other in the Baltic.

To the northwest of the Skaw, Denmark is separated from Norway by a narrow channel called the Skagerrak. To the east, the sheltered approach to the islands between Jutland and Sweden is called the Kattegat.

Much of western Jutland looks as flat as a pancake, with expanses of broad, sandy heaths, spongy peat bogs and empoldered marshes interspersed between tracts of well-tended farmland. Behind the North Sea beaches, the longest in Europe, is a rampart of sand dunes, driven eastward by powerful western winds and only prevented from engulfing the farmland by belts of protective conifers. In contrast, eastern Jutland has a hilly topography. Long inlets penetrate from the Kattegat, leading into steep-sided valleys where there are chains of lakes and woods of oak and beech. Farther inland is Denmark's highest point, Yding Skovhøj (Yding Forest Mountain). But this "mountain" reaches a height of less than 600 feet. As Danish novelist Martin A. Hansen has written, Denmark is so lacking in high points offering extensive views that the smallness of the country is less apparent to the eye.

Despite its modest relief, the countryside of Jutland offers a landscape of many moods with its sturdy beech woods, its stiff plantations of pine, its patchwork of arable lands, lush green meadows and purple summer heaths, its diked marshlands and soft-flowing streams, its trim villages with neat, whitewashed red-tiled farmhouses overlooking well-stocked gardens. Following reclamation of heathland and peat bogs in the 19th century, most of the land was put to agricultural use. But the peninsula also has well-developed industries, especially in and around its principal port of Esbjerg on the west coast, the city of Aalborg in the north, and Aarhus, Denmark's second-largest city, commonly called Jutland's capital on the east coast.

At the once-fortified town of Fredericia, south of Aarhus, two large bridges span the narrow strip of water, known as the Little Belt, which divides Jutland from the fertile island of Funen in the east. From these bridges, Funen — the so-called Garden of Denmark — is crossed by a major highway that leads to the port and university town of Odense (Hans Christian Andersen's birthplace) and on to the east coast, where car and train ferries regularly ply the Great Belt, which separates Funen from Zealand. Danes dream that one day a bridge will span this divide, so completing the road link between Jutland and Greater Copenhagen, the major metropolitan area that accommodates about one third of Denmark's population.

Copenhagen, capital of Denmark since 1443 and now Scandinavia's most populous city, derived its initial wealth from the abundance of herring in the Sound, the broad channel between the island of Zealand and southwest Sweden. With its free port, its ferry traffic, its shipyards and its overseas connections, it is still a "merchant's harbor," the origin of its Danish and Swedish name, the Oresund.

Visually, Copenhagen is reminiscent of Amsterdam. There is a strong Dutch influence in its Renaissance architecture, and it is a city that is inviting to the pedestrian because of its profusion of courtyards, squares, public gardens, winding streets and alley-ways. True, it lacks the canals of Amsterdam. Nevertheless, its association with water is close, by way of the moats of former fortifications, ornamental pools and fountains, historic quays and long waterfronts — most notably the treelined Langelinje promenade, beside which the bronze Little Mermaid, inspired by a Hans Christian Andersen fairy story, sits on a sea-washed rock amid a colorful array of private yachts.

But more than to Amsterdam, Copenhagen has been likened to the capital of France. In the language of the tourist brochures, it is "the Paris of the North," and although foreign visitors may find that description extravagant, by Nordic standards it is not without justification. No other city in Scandinavia has such a lively, free-and-easy atmosphere or such a vigorous night life. Copenhagen's most celebrated playground is the Tivoli Gardens, which boasts a Chinese pagoda, Arabian-style "mosques," parading toy soldiers, a trapeze arena, side shows and fireworks displays. The city's social life is less restricted by laws and conventions than elsewhere. There are more bars and restaurants per capita than in the other Scandinavian capitals; there are fewer restrictions on the sale of alcohol; and there is generally far greater scope for hedonistic pursuits.

In Copenhagen, the Danes can be seen at their most outgoing, recalling the English writer Evelyn Waugh's description of them as "the most exhilarating people in Europe." They are the *bon vivants* of the Nordic community: a warm and gregarious people who relish the wry patter of their comedian Victor Borge and the witty poems of Piet Hein (Denmark's Ogden Nash). They are a people of hearty appetites, who submit to the temptations of glutinous cream pastries and the *smorrebrod,* the open-faced Danish sandwich, which balances a maximum of gustatory delights upon a minimum of rye bread. Also typically Danish are low-taxed cigars (commonly smoked by women as well as men), more than one hundred kinds of beer, "Peter Herring" cherry liqueur, and akvavit, a colorless spirit produced from potatoes or grain and flavored with caraway seeds.

Romantics tend to see Denmark in terms of its quainter images: Viking burial mounds on top of almost every hill and storks' nests on the chimney pots of farmhouses; whitewashed medieval churches, grand castles and prim manor houses; chimney sweeps in traditional top hats and scarlet-uniformed postmen on yellow bicycles; and the extremely popular Legoland Park, a lilliputian realm created in Jutland by the Danish manufacturers of the toy building bricks. There is a certain quaintness, too, in the style of Denmark's ancient monarchy, which has taken to the common bicycle without rejecting such trappings of the imperial past as the Order of the Elephant (a decoration reserved for royalty and heads of state) and the busbied, red-coated soldiers who parade outside the magnificent, baroque Amalienborg Palace, the royal family's principal residence in central Copenhagen.

For the connoisseur, Denmark brings to mind the Royal Copenhagen porcelain and glittering Georg Jensen silverware, stylish furniture fashioned from imported tropical wood, and a great range of high-quality fabrics and household goods. (The Danes have achieved the ultimate in qualitative advertising far and wide by using just three words on their billboards: "Good, Better, Danish.") More down-to-earth consumers are likely to identify Denmark with its remarkable output of agricultural products. It is the world's third-largest exporter of cheese, the second-largest exporter of butter and the largest exporter of bacon. Indeed, in Denmark, pigs outnumber people almost 2 to 1, and each year they provide approximately one million tons of pork and bacon.

Yet despite this wealth, only 7 percent of the population engages in agriculture, fishing and forestry; the overwhelming majority of citizens live by industry, trade and service activities. And despite their taste for the good life, Danes are hard workers. Only thus is it possible to explain the extremely high standard of living achieved by a

THE COLD TABLE: AN ABUNDANCE OF CHOICE

An array of cold dishes awaits patrons of Copenhagen's railroad station restaurant.

The Danish equivalent of the Swedish and Finnish *smörgäsbord* is the *kolde bord,* or "cold table." Prepared principally for lunch, it includes at least half a dozen types of pickled fish and as many kinds of spiced and smoked meats, accompanied by a selection of salads and *pâtés,* and sliced rye bread for making open-faced sandwiches.

1

country naturally deficient in raw materials and, unlike Norway, Sweden, Finland and Iceland, almost completely without its own sources of energy.

Although only 81 miles of water separates the northern tip of Denmark from the southern coast of Norway, the contrast between the two countries could hardly be more dramatic. Where the landscape of Denmark is widely cultivated, well ordered and low lying (Norwegians sometimes refer to the Danes as Flatlanders), most of Norway's landscape is stark and rugged, almost primeval in aspect. Four fifths of its more than 125,180-square-mile territory is at least 490 feet above sea level. It is one of the most mountainous countries in Europe — "Switzerland by the sea," as Honoré de Balzac described it. Physically, it is also one of the least developed Scandinavian countries, with less than 3 percent of its land under cultivation.

Norway's shape — curving in a scenic arc of mountains, forests and fjords along the western side of Sweden — has been likened to that of a crouched lion, with its massive head and shoulders in the west, its forefeet in the southeast, and its long extended tail ending in a curl on the borders of the Soviet Union and Finland in the far north. With almost half of its length lying within the Arctic Circle, it can claim the world's most northerly town (Hammerfest) and the most northerly university (at Tromso). Among other distinctions, it has Europe's deepest lake (1,600-foot-deep Lake Hornindal) and largest mountain plateau (4,000-square-mile Hardangervidda); the world's deepest fjord (4,000-foot-deep Sogne Fjord), and several waterfalls that are among the highest in the world.

The most significant feature of this rugged, elongated land, however, is its intimate relationship with the sea. Henrik Ibsen, Norway's supreme dramatist once said that Norwegians were "hypnotized by the water." This is no surprise, because about 75 percent of its people live within sight of the coast. In addition, the country boasts numerous lakes, countless energy-producing mountain rivers and waterfalls, and scores of fjords, including two — Sogne Fjord and Hardanger Fjord — which penetrate as far as 100 miles inland. It is estimated that if all the fjords were straightened out, Norway's coastline of approximately 2,100 miles would be stretched to 12,497 miles, more than half the circumference of the earth.

Norway's name is born of the sea. It springs from a Norse word meaning "northern way," and refers to the 600-mile-long sea lane, sheltered by skerries and islands, which extends from Stavanger in the southwest to Tromso in the north. For centuries, overland transport routes were so limited and hazardous that this offshore passage was the critical link between the widely scattered communities. Modern road, rail and air communications have lessened the importance of this seaway, but water is still a key influence on the life of the nation. Norway is a major shipping power. It also draws a rich harvest of fish from the sea, and gains an even richer harvest in the form of the North Sea oil and gas.

Most significantly, water has revolutionized life in Norway by yielding an abundance of hydroelectric power. No

country in the world has a greater wealth of water-driven energy in relation to its population. And this resource has greatly accelerated the rate of industrialization and urbanization. Less than a century ago, most of the Norwegian working population derived its living from fishing, forestry and farming. Today, the figure is less than 10 percent. The overwhelming majority of workers are now engaged in industry and service activities, and more than 70 percent of the population inhabits towns.

Norway is divided traditionally into five regions: lofty Vestlandet (Westland) in the southwest; wooded Östlandet (Eastland) in the southeast; sheltered Sorlandet (Southland), which extends along the Skagerrak coast; the more open land of the Trondelag area in the center; and Nord-Norge (Northern Norway), most of which lies north of the Arctic Circle. Following industrialization at the turn of the century, there has been a continuous drift of workers from the north to the cities of the south. More than half of Norway's 4.1 million population now lives in Östlandet, and the majority are concentrated in and around Oslo, the capital and the most important industrial, commercial and shipping center.

The city of Oslo lies at the head of a 69-mile-long fjord opening onto the Skagerrak, thus giving sea access to Norway's principal trading partners—southern Sweden, Denmark, Germany, the Netherlands and Britain. The old fortress of Akershus overlooks the capital's deep-water harbor, which can accommodate the ships of cruise lines; and within shouting distance of Oslo's monumental town hall is a wharf where oil tankers of more than 250,000 tons have been built. The center of the city

On the Danish island of Zealand, fields of yellow rape, grown for animal feed and vegetable oil, surround neat, whitewashed farmhouses. With approximately 70 percent of its land used for farming, Denmark is the most agricultural country in Scandinavia.

1

is dominated by the neoclassical royal palace, which was built in the early 19th century and stands on high ground in a large, triangular-shaped park. Another park — far more famous (or infamous) — lies little more than a mile away. This is Frogner Park, for which the sculptor Gustav Vigeland spent more than three decades creating an elaborate arrangement of sculpture: hundreds of statues, mainly nudes, in all manner of shapes, sizes and postures. It is all on a staggering scale. Evelyn Waugh — no admirer of the sculptor's work — uncompromisingly described it as "a multitudinous subhuman zoo . . . far more awful than the ruins of Hiroshima."

In contrast to the more densely populated Östlandet, Vestlandet is the Norway of the travel brochures: leaping waterfalls, glaciers, innumerable off-shore islands and skerries (Norwegians say they stopped counting at 50,000), and mountain flanks dropping in precipices to the sea, as if alpine peaks had been transported down to the east coast and then sliced open with some enormous cheesecutter. And in the far west, Bergen — which is arguably the most picturesque city in Scandinavia — the lofty works of nature blend supremely with the monuments of humankind.

Bergen was once the capital of Norway, and until 1800, it was also the largest city. Now, although its population has been outpaced by that of Oslo, Bergen remains the cultural heart of Verslandet, and it is still distinguished by a style of its own. The Hanseatic harbor, filled with shipping and surrounded by a bustling open-air market, is backed by tiers of brightly painted clapboard houses. The construction of a funicular railway, climbing to the top of Mount Floyen behind the town, has made more accessible the spectacular views that once inspired the Norwegian composer Edvard Grieg, whose lakeside summer home, Troll Hill, stands on the outskirts of the city.

Verslandet also takes in Norway's fourth-largest industrial center with a fine peninsular setting. Since the opening of the North Sea fields at the beginning of the 1970s, this pleasant town of wooden, pantiled houses has become the nation's oil capital, a construction and supply base, and something of a boom town, accommodating an international community and immigrants from all over Norway.

Trondelag is centered on the broad Trondheim Fjord, where farm and forest country embrace Norway's third-largest city, Trondheim, the seat of the archbishopric of Norway. Its Gothic-style cathedral is the burial place of Norwegian kings. More significantly, as a major communications center, Trondheim is at the fulcrum of Norway, so central that the Germans, during their occupation in World War II, planned to make it the national capital.

North Norway comprises the three counties of Nordland, Troms and Finnmark. The forest mantle is restricted to the sheltered dales, farming is limited, and the fisheries take precedence. Cod is the most valuable harvest — caught in vast quantities off the nearby Lofoten Islands in late winter and off the north coast in summer. The northernmost counties of Finnmark and Troms contain most of Norway's reindeer-herding Laplanders, whose animals move by the thousand down to the coast for grazing in the summertime. Today, only a minority of Lapps move with them. Most are settled on small farmsteads.

The largest towns in north Norway are Bodø on the Vest Fjord; Mo i Rana, a major iron- and steel-producing center; Narvik, the iron-ore terminal that was prominent during World War II operations; and Tromso, a university town and the site of the Cathedral of the Arctic. Tromso is also a traditional base for expeditions to the Arctic, and the terminal point for air and sea transport linking mainland Norway with Svalbard, the bleak archipelago approximately 400 miles to the north that includes the island of Spitsbergen. In 1920, an international treaty accorded Norway sovereignty over the archipelago, and granted the 41 signatories of the treaty equal access to the island for maritime, industrial, mining and commercial purposes. Today, some 2,000 Soviets take advantage of their treaty right, vying with about 1,000 Norwegians, who brave the island's harsh climate to mine almost 500,000 tons of coal a year.

The Norwegians, of course, are well accustomed to such challenging environments. The isolation imposed on them by mountains, wastelands and forests, the imprisoning world of fjords and dales and long, dark winters — these are factors that put a premium on self-reliance. Norway's heroes are people who stubbornly defy all odds in pursuit of their goals: men like Fridtjof Nansen, the polar explorer; Roald Amundsen, the first man to reach the South Pole; and the modern-day Viking, Thor Heyerdahl, who drifted for 101 days on the fragile balsawood raft Kon-Tiki to corroborate a theory that Polynesia could have been settled by South Americans.

Living so close to an untamed, awesome environment has also invested many Norwegians with a keen sense of

Two Lapp women in traditional costume *(below)* lay out bundles of braided trimming for sale at a Lapp festival in northern Finland. Men's clothing is also richly embroidered and features elaborate, silver-studded belts *(right)*.

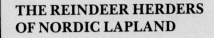

THE REINDEER HERDERS OF NORDIC LAPLAND

In the Arctic and sub-Arctic areas of northern Norway, Sweden and Finland live an estimated 50,000 Lapps, an indigenous people with a rich and distinctive heritage. Known as *sami* in their language, the Lapps evolved a seminomadic lifestyle and survived for centuries by herding reindeer, fishing, hunting and fur trading.

Today, most Lapps are well integrated into Scandinavian society, but are increasingly assertive about their culture, their language and territorial rights. About 10 percent continue to herd reindeer, helped by such modern conveniences as snowmobiles, two-way radios and even helicopters. Most other Lapps are settled on small farms, where they eke out a living as part-time or seasonal workers. In addition, most families keep one or two cows, a few sheep and some domesticated reindeer, and they cultivate a patch of land on which they grow potatoes and oats.

Outside a Lapp homestead in northern Norway, a snowmobile stands beside a trailer carrying a sledge — a traditional Lapp conveyance once commonly drawn by reindeer. In the background, deerskins — eventually to be sold as rugs — are hung out to dry on the walls of a wooden outbuilding.

Lofty antlers provide an easy target for a young Lapp lassoing a reindeer in an annual roundup. There are more than one million of the deer in Lapland, of which about a fifth are slaughtered yearly. Meat accounts for 90 percent of an animal's cash value, with bone, horn and hide accounting for the rest.

the supernatural. Generation after generation of imaginative storytellers have populated Norway with water sprites and witches, sea serpents and trolls. More significant, the magical atmosphere has been a powerful source of inspiration to novelists, painters, poets and composers, who have sought to capture the unique spirit of place that is manifest in so many parts of the country. When the 19th-century violinist Ole Bull, who enchanted European audiences with his performances of Norwegian folk melodies, was asked by the king of Denmark who had taught him to play, Bull simply replied: "The Norwegian mountains, your Majesty." The supreme statement of this Norwegian romanticism is Henrik Ibsen's *Peer Gynt,* which gathers together a whole tribe of supernatural creatures around a central character who is the apotheosis of individualism.

In general, the Norwegian people are fairly conservative in their outlook with a strong streak of puritanism. There are no newspapers or alcohol on sale in Norway on the sabbath; and significantly, the country was slower than its Danish and Swedish neighbors to accept legalized abortion and sex education. On the other hand, the people have a spontaneous sense of fun and a great love of sport. As visiting foreigners have often observed, most Norwegians seem to have achieved a high standard of living without becoming slaves to materialism and without losing sight of human values.

Like all the Scandinavian countries, Norway is a parliamentary democracy, with the legislative power vested in the 150-strong Storting (Parliament). The king is a figurehead, taking no part in political issues. In modern times, all the royal children have married common-

ers—unsurprisingly, since there have been no titled families other than royalty in Norway since 1821, when the parliament voted to abolish nobility. Many years later, Ibsen remarked that "Norwegians can only agree on one point—to drag down the lofty." The result has been the most egalitarian society in mainland Europe.

Although it shares a 1,030-mile-long border with Norway, Sweden has more in common physically with its other immediate neighbor, Finland, which it faces across the brackish Gulf of Bothnia in the east and across a 360-mile-long land frontier in the north. To be sure, Sweden sometimes brings to mind Norway's scenic magnificence, with deep valleys, great waterfalls and, in Swedish Lapland, mountain peaks that rise more than 6,500 feet high. For the most part, however, Sweden is relatively low lying, and like Finland, it has myriad lakes and rivers and vast coniferous forests.

This is the largest country in Scandinavia, and the fourth-largest in Europe. Its varied landscapes, ranging from modest glaciers in the far north to sandy beaches in the southwest, are largely explained by the fact that it extends some 980 miles latitudinally. In the southwestern province of Skane—rich farmland with broad open fields of autumn wheat, glossy-leafed sugar beets and other arable crops—Sweden also shares topographical characteristics with Denmark. It is popularly said by Swedes that God gave Skane to Sweden to show them what the rest of Europe looks like.

Perhaps the most distinctive feature of Sweden is the fact that almost all settlement is water oriented, either coastal, lakeside or riverside. An impressive

Yachts from the nearby Danish port of Helsingor sweep past Kronborg Castle, a Renaissance stronghold overlooking the choppy Oresund. For more than 400 years, until 1857, tolls were levied on all foreign ships passing through the channel, at its narrowest here, two and a half miles from Sweden.

series of parallel rivers cross the northern half of the country diagonally, disgorging through waterfalls and rapids from the mountain lakes on the Norwegian border to the shallow estuaries on the Bothnian Sea. And lakes of all sizes — at least 90,000 of them — are scattered throughout the land. Some are so large that the early inhabitants regarded them as inland seas. They include the third-largest lake in Europe, the 2,142-square-mile Lake Vaner, which is linked to the west-coast city of Gothenburg by the Gota Canal.

This marriage of land and water is further emphasized by the infinitely fragmented character of the generally low-lying Swedish coasts. They are rich in archipelagos, some of them of extraordinary complexity. For example, the hundreds of wooded islands at the approaches to Stockholm provide a veritable maze of waterside escapes for the Swedish people to enjoy in summer. In contrast, there are innumerable wave-swept, granite islands in the exposed archipelago of the western region of Bohuslän.

Sweden also has two islands of notable size. Off the southeastern coast, the long, narrow limestone island of Öland is connected to the historic mainland city of Kalmar by a magnificent bridge 3.77 miles long and with more than 150 piers. Beyond Öland, in the middle of the Baltic, lies Sweden's largest island, Gotland, with its fabled, walled capital of Visby, the most impressive medieval town in all Scandinavia. Once a Viking stronghold and later Sweden's richest trading center, Gotland is now primarily a farming community, and it is such a popular tourist resort that in summer visitors outnumber the island population of 54,000 by about 4 to 1.

1

On the mainland, trees rival lakes and rivers as the dominant feature of the Swedish countryside. There were 51 billion of them at the last estimate, varying from white-barked birch and dark-green pine and spruce forests in the north to beech and oak woods in the southwest. Sweden boasts the largest softwood timber reserves in all of Europe, and together with Finland, its woodlands — covering more than half the nation's land area — are more carefully managed than those of any other country in the world.

Being relatively rich in mineral resources — especially iron and other basic ores — Sweden has always been the most industrialized of the Nordic countries. It is also the most urbanized. About 90 percent of the population of 8.3 million now live in the southern half of the country, the greatest concentrations being in the major metropolitan areas of Stockholm, Gothenburg and Malmo. Of these, Stockholm is by far the largest, with more than 1.5 million residents. It is also more centrally located in relation to its country than any other Nordic capital.

Stockholm (the name means a stockaded island, or *holm*) was founded in the 13th century at the narrows where Lake Malar meets the Baltic Sea. The city is so interlaced with waterways that it has, inevitably, been called "the Venice of the North"; and although the de-

A passenger ferry sails past several of the 24,000 or more islands in the Baltic that constitute the Stockholm archipelago. Romantically named the Skägård, or "Garden of Skerries," these islands are peppered with thousands of summer homes occupied by Swedes on weekends and for vacations.

scription is a little ambitious it is at least supported by many spires and domes, old and new, by a wealth of baroque architecture, by an attractive neo-Romantic city hall, and by the city's many bridges and waterside walks and piazzas. Much of the Old Town of Stockholm, having escaped both war and fires is intact, with its original marketplace and maze of narrow cobbled streets lined with gabled buildings, many of which now house antique shops. The trappings of monarchy still exist in its Renaissance-style royal palace. In the chapels of the city's medieval Riddarholm Church, once part of a monastery, are the tombstones of every Swedish monarch since 1632 with the exception of Queen Christina, who was converted to Roman Catholicism and eventually buried in Rome.

Apart from its archipelago and its waterways, the greatest recreational assets in Stockholm are its parks and open spaces. Kungstradgården, the Royal Garden close by the palace, is the most centrally located. To the east are Ladugården and Djurgården (Deer Park). The latter was a royal hunting preserve from the 16th to the 18th century, but it is now most renowned as the site of Scandinavia's oldest and largest outdoor museum, Skansen. Designed to preserve examples of life in preindustrial Sweden, Skansen contains scores of historic buildings that have been transplanted from various parts of the country. They include a church and a manor house, Lapp dwellings, peasant farmhouses, and workshops in which old crafts such as butter and cheese making, weaving, wood turning and glass blowing are demonstrated. In addition, Skansen has a zoo, restaurants and a summer theater.

On the west coast, a four-hour trip by

In central Stockholm's Vasastan district, apartment houses constructed at the turn of the century stretch out like ticker tape in the sun. The buildings, which house mainly middle-class families, are built around two, or sometimes even three, courtyards.

train from Stockholm, is Gothenburg, Sweden's largest seaport and second-largest city. In this breezy metropolis, the atmosphere is noticeably different: more extroverted and vigorous, reflecting its North Sea outlook. Approximately 40 percent of Sweden's merchant fleet is harbored at Gothenburg. From the lofty suspension bridge that spans its busy Gota River may be seen the impressive factories that produce Volvo cars and trucks, Mölnlycke textiles, and the steel products of SKF, one of the world's leading producers of ball bearings.

The citizens of Gothenburg regard themselves as being essentially independent of their far-off capital in the east. Malmo, Sweden's third-largest city in the extreme south, is even farther from Stockholm. It is connected to the Copenhagen area by a constant shuttle of ferries and hydrofoils across the Sound, so its citizens have a closer association with the Danish capital than with Stockholm. Nevertheless, a recognizably similar lifestyle unites most of the inhabitants of the nation's populous southern provinces. Indeed, in all of

Sweden's leading cities, most people live in well-designed, ultramodern high-rise apartment buildings. Yet whenever possible, they will escape to the countryside, often staying in primitive wooden dwellings without plumbing and far away from public services. The yearning for the great outdoors is partly compensatory, because Sweden is one of the most developed countries in the world. Affluence is manifest everywhere. Sweden is near the top of international tables for the ownership of automobiles, television sets, refrigerators and telephones; and the nation's gross national product is rivaled only by Switzerland and Norway among European countries.

Sweden's prosperity is the product of a mixed economy. Long ago, the nation developed a social order described as "the middle way" between capitalism and socialism. Some economic sectors — for example, railroads, post offices and telecommunications — are state owned, but about 90 percent of Swedish industry is in private hands. At the same time, the cooperative movement thrives on a greater scale than in

HELSINKI'S BUSTLING WATERFRONT MARKET

A colorful feature of Helsinki life is the open-air market on the spacious waterfront of the South Harbor. It operates from 7 a.m. to 2 p.m. every Monday to Saturday, except in midwinter. When the waterways are free of ice, Finns from outlying islands tie up their boats along the quay and sell a wide range of home-grown produce, as well as salmon, whitefish, herring and crayfish. In addition, waterside stalls offer cut flowers and potted plants for sale, along with such household goods as brooms, baskets, braided rugs — and that indispensable feature of the Finnish sauna, the birch whisk.

A man sells carrots from a market booth.

Smoked herring is displayed on a boat.

A boat owner sells flowers, potatoes and fresh dill from the stern of his launch. In the background, stalls crowd the waterfront.

most other European countries, and about 80 percent of the work force belongs to a labor union.

Although the left-of-center Social Democratic party was in power almost continously from 1932 to 1976, it never made a fetish of nationalization. By the same token, industrial and trade policy did not undergo any fundamental change after 1976 when a nonsocialist coalition Cabinet was formed. Swedish governments have avoided extreme political stances. Instead, they have concentrated their efforts, with a large measure of success, on promoting economic growth and sustaining as far as possible a well-established system of social welfare — the most advanced of its kind in the world.

To an even greater degree than neighboring Sweden, Finland is a country of woodland and water. On a large-scale map, it looks like a jigsaw puzzle two-thirds completed on a table of blue. The gaps are lakes — approximately 62,000 of them, ranging from small, lonely forest pools visited only by elk and crane to great sheets of inland water such as Saimaa, the fifth-largest lake in Europe. To expand the simile, the unused pieces scattered around the jigsaw puzzle would be Finland's tens of thousands of offshore islands and islets, of which some 7,000 constitute the Åland archipelago, an autonomous province that is situated midway between Finland and Sweden.

In summer, the dominant color of this fragmented country is green — not the bright acid green of cultivated land, which accounts for less than 10 percent of Finland's 130,000 square miles, but the dark, boreal hues of pine and spruce forests, which spread over nearly 70 percent of the territory. This is

Europe's most forested country. Only above the Arctic Circle do the trees begin to peter out, to be replaced by great tracts of moors, bogs and fells dotted with lichen-covered outcrops of the granite shield that underlies the thin soil. Almost everywhere else, the forest closes in, tranquil and melancholy, hypnotic and monotonous, blanketing the low ridges and hills.

In the treeless northwest there are mountains 3,300 feet high, but in many other areas of Finland the only way to see the forest from the trees is to climb the high ridges of sand and gravel that, like eccentric railroad embankments, snake over the landscape. Called eskers, these ridges were deposited by the ice sheet that buried Finland 10,000 years ago. At the same time, the ice created thousands of lakes by scouring hollows in the land. Finland has still not recovered from the Ice Age — literally, since in some areas the land is rising from the sea at the rate of more than 30 inches a century as it regains its geological equilibrium after shedding its glacial burden.

Geographically, this is one of the northernmost countries in the world: It has approximately one third of its land within the Arctic Circle. In the north, the first snows often fall in late September, blizzards may strike well into May, and mean temperatures are likely to remain below 23° F. for 160 days or more. The rigorous climate helps to explain why a country about 40 percent larger than Britain has only 4.8 million inhabitants, compared with 56 million in Britain. More precisely, it indicates why two thirds of the Finnish population is settled in the southern third of the country. There, in urban municipalities, the population density is 210.6 inhabitants per square mile whereas in Lappi, the

largest and most northern of Finland's 12 provinces, it is only 3.1 people per square mile.

Almost one million Finns — one fifth of the population — live in Helsinki's metropolitan area. Another quarter of a million live in and around the city of Turku, the capital until 1812 and still the ecclesiastical center of the Evangelical Lutheran Church, to which more than 90 percent of the population belongs. Tampere, a thriving industrial center about 100 miles northwest of Helsinki, is Finland's other big city; the rest of the urban population — 60 percent of the total — live in towns with fewer than 90,000 inhabitants.

Less than 15 percent of the population is now engaged in farming and forestry, as opposed to some 50 percent in 1950. However, despite a steady drift from villages to towns, Finland is not as intensively urbanized as most other industrialized countries. There are still many small industrial communities, and even the loneliest traveler is likely at some time to catch sight of the smokestack of an isolated paper mill, or see a great raft of tree trunks on a lake, at the start of a journey to the timber mills and workshops that produce more than one third of the nation's export earnings.

In Finland, as in Sweden and Norway, almost all towns have waterfront settings that, together with their spacious layouts and generous areas of parkland, make them appear large in proportion to their populations. This is even true of Helsinki, the cultural and commercial heart of the country. Helsinki is Finland's largest industrial city and its busiest port, a capital whose many monumental buildings are concentrated in the neoclassical core and surrounded by high-rise residential districts. Its many parks, broad boulevards and seafront promenades give the city an air of spaciousness. Even so, there is never quite space enough for the country-loving Finn. Like Sweden's capital, Helsinki tends to empty in summertime, especially on weekends, as tens of thousands of city dwellers make an exodus to waterside cottages and forest cabins, all of which are equipped with their own sauna — *de rigueur* for most of the population.

It is a migration pattern common to all of Finland. Whenever possible, the people like to escape the urban areas: In summer, they boat, fish, swim or pick berries; in autumn, they gather mushrooms and hunt elk or deer; in winter, they take to their skis. As a native of Helsinki expresses it, "Scratch a Finn and you find an animist. We want to go into the forest, to be alone and have a private dialogue with nature."

Such a yearning for solitude constitutes something of a paradox. As individuals, living in such a spacious, tranquil land, the Finns seek their own remote, isolated worlds. As a nation, however, they have always been haunted by a sense of isolation. This is largely the result of history and geography. Unlike the Danes, Norwegians and Swedes, the Finns took little or no part in the far-ranging Viking explorations of a thousand years ago. For more than 600 years, from the 13th century until 1809, Finland was part of Sweden and often served as a buffer to Russian aggression. It then became a Grand Duchy of Russia until gaining independence in 1917. As European tourism developed, foreigners increasingly traveled to Denmark, Norway and Sweden, but Finland lay off the tourists' track until more recent years.

More particularly, the Finnish sense

of isolation has been fostered by a language that is unrelated to any Norse tongue or to Russian. Finnish, like Estonian and Lappish, belongs to the Finno-Ugric family of languages, supporting the theory that the Finns are descendants of peoples who had their origin near the Ural Mountains and moved westward in a series of migrations starting about 4,000 years ago. Because of the language barrier, the nation has suffered from a degree of cultural isolation. To be sure, some achievements have transcended the barrier. Through music — most notably that of Sibelius — Finland has found a universal voice, while through the works of Alvar Aalto and other outstanding architects, Finland has acquired designs for living that have been adopted by many countries. But its considerable literary achievements have gone largely unrecognized. Apart from translations of the great Finnish folk epic *Kalevala,* Finnish literature remains unknown to most of the world.

One way in which the sense of isolation manifests itself today is in an obsessive concern about the overseas image of Finland and its people. As Erkki Toivanen, the Paris correspondent for the Finnish Broadcasting Company, explained: "Finns are obsessed about the knowledge, or lack of it, others have of our country. Now that what used to be Europe is divided into 'Europe,' Soviet bloc, and Scandinavia, we are desperately trying to impress the Scandinavishness of Finland on foreigners. It is of vital importance to our self-esteem that people know where we live, who we are ruled by, and under what kind of system."

Finland's institutions are Western European. Its educational system follows the German model; its rural cooperative structures have been inspired by those of Denmark; its legal, administrative and constitutional systems are cast in the Swedish mold. And this parliamentary republic is headed by a democratically elected president whose powers are largely based upon those of the president of the United States.

For all their Western-style institutions, however, the Finns cannot afford to ignore the necessity of maintaining a respectful relationship with the Soviets.

In the hotel at Mundal, a Norwegian village nestling on an arm of the Sogne Fjord, guests at a wedding reception drink a toast to the bride and groom. Most of the women are dressed in folk costume — a practice that is still widespread on festive occasions.

Only China and Mongolia have a longer frontier with the Soviet Union. Over the centuries, Finland has fought numerous wars against the Russians and lost every one of them. The last bitter conflict, from 1941 to 1944, cost the Finns 10 percent of their land, including the country's only outlet to the Arctic Sea, and 300 million dollars' worth of reparations. Recently, it has been estimated that Finland's military establishment — strictly organized on defensive lines — is one three-hundredth the size of the Soviet Union's. And it is a sobering thought that in the city of Leningrad alone — less than 100 miles over the border — there are more Soviet citizens than there are Finns in the whole of Finland.

It is little wonder then that the 1948 Soviet-Finnish Treaty of Friendship, Cooperation and Mutual Assistance has been twice extended (now until the year 2003) and that Finnish leaders consistently eschew criticism of Soviet politics. Finland endeavors to maintain a strict neutrality in its East-West affairs, and to give equal attention to fostering good relations with both capitalist and Communist countries. By and large, it has managed to sustain good will in both spheres with a high degree of success. Its diplomatic dexterity is exemplified by its purchase of armaments: Finland buys one third of its defense weaponry from the Soviet Union, one third from the West, and one third from either neutral countries or its own arms industries.

Finland has also contrived to turn its dual relationships to economic advantage. By means of a series of five-year agreements, it has provided the Soviet Union — its biggest single trading partner — with ships and industrial goods in exchange for oil and natural gas. At the same time, Finland has developed strong economic links with the West through the Nordic Council, the Organization for Economic Cooperation and Development (OECD), EFTA, and free-trade agreements with the EEC. This unique trading position helped Finland to weather the world recession in the 1970s. Indeed, by the mid-1980s, Finland was showing the fastest growth rate among members of the OECD, even surpassing that of Japan.

Attempting to explain to Westerners the pragmatic nature of their country's neutrality, Finnish officials sometimes relate an old anecdote dating from the civil war of 1918, when Red Guards (pro-Bolshevik Finns aided by Russian revolutionaries) were ranged against White Guards (anti-Bolshevik Finns aided by German troops). A man standing on the Tampere bridge after dark suddenly felt the barrel of a soldier's rifle pressed into the small of his back. "Red or white?" the soldier demanded.

"May I first know who is asking?" countered the civilian.

The Finns face up to their position on the tightrope between East and West with fortitude. The quality they most admire is *sisu* — a composite word meaning "courage," "resilience," the "refusal to accept defeat." *Sisu* has made the Finns eminent in the more grueling forms of sporting competition such as long-distance running and skiing, and marathon auto rallies. It is the quality that has contributed above all others to Finland's emergence and survival as an independent nation.

Unlike the Finns, or indeed any of their Nordic neighbors, the people of Iceland have never experienced war directly. Yet, in their own way, they also deserve to be characterized in terms of

Jokingly dressed in an outsize jacket and top hat, a boy in Oslo clutches a flag as he joins in the celebrations of Norway's national day. On the 17th of May every year, the anniversary of the Constitution of 1814 is marked by processions and ceremonies on a scale unequaled in Scandinavia.

sisu, having contended with awesome forces. For centuries, the Icelanders have had to struggle for survival on a remote island constantly ravaged by volcanic eruptions and earthquakes — as well as famine and disease. Their country remains the most volcanically active land in Europe, and it is still subject to earthquakes.

A vivid reminder of Iceland's violent history came on the morning of the 14th of November, 1963, when the crew of an Icelandic fishing boat sighted a huge column of black smoke rising far out to sea. Presuming a ship to be in distress, they raced to the rescue. Instead, they found a position — about 17 miles off the southwest coast of Iceland — where the sea had become a boiling caldron from which billowed great clouds of ash and vapor. The following day, a black cone of lava rose

almost 35 feet above the seething waters and sent lumps of red-hot rock flying into the steam-filled air. For more than two years, volcanic eruptions continued, in the process creating an island more than one square mile in size. Icelanders called their new offshore territory "Surtsey," after Surtur, the fire-making giant of Norse legend.

With such spectacle and fury, on an infinitely larger scale and over millions of years, Iceland itself was created — born of fire out of water. In the course of countless eruptions, it has grown to its present-day size of 39,700 square miles, making it, after Greenland and Britain, the third-largest island in Europe. Historically, it is one of the older nations of the world; yet it also remains one of the smallest, with fewer than 300,000 inhabitants.

This land of legends is believed to have been first settled by Irish monks in the eighth century. However, according to *Landnambok,* the nation's historic *Book of Settlements,* compiled in the 13th century, the Norwegian chieftain Ingolfur Arnarson was the first permanent settler in the year 874. The story claims that, when in sight of land, he threw the wooden pillars of his ancestral Norwegian home into the sea, vowing that he would settle where they came ashore. Three years later, he found the pillars in a little bay that he named Reykjavik, or "Bay of Smoke." Whatever the historical accuracy of the tale, it has always been dear to the Icelanders, who have seen the hidden hand of fate in Reykjavik's emergence as Iceland's capital and principal center of population.

An earlier Viking explorer, Floki Vigerdarson, is credited with having disparagingly coined the name "Iceland," after judging the land unfit for human

Three of the guards assigned to the royal palace in central Oslo relax outside the adjoining guardhouse before going on duty. The ceremonial uniforms are the star attraction of the changing of the guard, which takes place in front of the palace.

habitation. It was a misleading choice. About 11.7 percent of the island's surface is covered by glaciers, and Vatnajökull, more than 3,200 square miles, is the largest in Europe; but ice is by no means the dominant characteristic. A far more accurate title would have been "Lavaland," for basaltic rocks and solidified lava — cooled and eroded into weird shapes — provide much of the island's fantastic scenery.

Altogether, Iceland has some 200 volcanoes known to have been active in postglacial times. Of these, more than 20 are still active, the most celebrated being Mount Hekla, once so fiery that medieval writers identified it as one of the main gates to hell. Contrastingly, the most beautiful of all the volcanic peaks is Snaefell, whose Fujiyama-like profile can be seen on a clear day in Reykjavik, almost hanging in the air some 70 miles away across Faxa Bay. It was down the throat of Snaefell that Jules Verne's fictional heroes made their journey to the center of the earth.

An eruption of some kind occurs in this country roughly once every five years. The last time volcanic activity caused serious damage was in January 1973, when the entire 5,300-plus population of Heimaey, the only inhabited island in Iceland's offshore Westman group, had to be evacuated within a few hours of the first rumble. The eruption lasted for more than three months and left the island's only town, Vestmannaeyjar, half-submerged in lava and half-buried in ashes.

As a result of centuries of eruptions, much of Iceland has a bald, open appearance and is so naked of trees that even modest areas of birch scrub are graced with the description of "woodland." The scenery in the vast, uninhabited interior conjures up images of lunar landscapes; indeed, in the mid-1960s, American astronauts were flown there so that they could familiarize themselves with the kind of terrain likely to be encountered on the moon. Mainly, this terrain is made up of extensive ash deserts, some of them relics of the great eruption of 1783 that destroyed thousands of animals, poisoned vegetation and grazing lands, created a famine that ultimately caused the deaths of about 25,000 people and, at its peak, shot dust so high into the atmosphere that the effects were recorded by Benjamin Franklin, who was in Paris, 1,200 miles away.

Everywhere, there are constant reminders of the tremendous natural power that lies beneath the earth's surface. They take the form of bubbling mud pools, hundreds of hot springs and, most spectacularly, the famous Great Geysir, from which the English word "geyser" derives. Hot springs provide central heating for 80 percent of all houses in Iceland, supply warm water for nearly 30 outdoor swimming pools, and they sustain tropical greenhouses in which tomatoes, grapes, melons, pineapples, bananas and even coffee beans are grown.

Inevitably, this harsh and rugged land has forged a tough and resilient people. Its isolation — the nearest neighbor is Scotland, more than 450 miles away — has also been a significant influence. Left to their own devices, far removed from the mainstream of European development, the Icelanders have forged a remarkably homogeneous and egalitarian society, undivided by variations in race, creed or tongue. The language has changed relatively little in structure or sound from that of the ninth-century settlers, and Icelanders claim that it is the oldest in common

everyday use in the world. This tradition is so cherished that leading academicians search for obsolete words that may be revived with new meanings. For example, *simi,* meaning "long thread," is now used for "telephone."

Iceland's remoteness was effectively ended by the opening of regular air-passenger services after World War II. In 1950, the country was visited by 5,000 foreigners; by the mid-1980s, the number of tourists had increased more than tenfold. Iceland was also drawn more and more into the international arena as a member of the United Nations, EFTA, OECD, the Council of Europe, NATO and the Nordic Council. Meanwhile, in the wake of industrialization, Icelanders have become much less isolated within their own country. In the two decades following World War II, the country was transformed from an essentially rural and agricultural society into an urbanized society with an industrial economy. Today, almost two thirds of the people live in the climatically favored southwest, in or near Reykjavik, and manufacturing and services now employ a large part of the working population.

Nevertheless, fishing remains critical to the economic life of Iceland, and it accounts for about 75 percent of all exports. Only about 1 percent of the land is cultivated. The climate restricts crops to grass, oats and potatoes. Accordingly, animal husbandry is foremost in agriculture, to the extent that Iceland is self-sufficient in meat, poultry and dairy products. Sheep, above all, dominate the rural scene — more than 750,000 of them, kept out of the fields and gardens by Iceland's ubiquitous fencing material, barbed wire. They are herded on the grazing lands with the aid of the island's distinctive ponies, which are hardy enough to withstand the inclement climate, sure-footed enough to cover the rough countryside, and so small that their height is measured in thumbs instead of hands.

Although the majority of Icelanders now live in a modern, urbanized society, they remain doggedly traditional and conservative, jealously guarding their culture and ever wary of foreign influence. The existence of a big American NATO base at Keflavik, 30 miles west of the capital, has been a subject of controversy ever since it was es-

Boxlike houses with brightly painted tin roofs surround Lake Tjornin in the heart of Reykjavik, the capital city of Iceland. Reykjavik and nearby settlements accommodate some 120,000 people, more than 50 percent of Iceland's total population.

tablished in 1951. It has provided a valuable boost to the national economy, and yet, in 1980, Iceland's newly elected first woman president, Vigdis Finnbogadottir, described the base as "an unpleasant necessity." By the same token, Iceland's state-owned radio and television are on guard against foreign words that might creep into common usage and dilute the purity of the Icelandic language. Warnings against such intrusions are frequently broadcast. More positively, there are weekly readings on radio of sagas and Eddas, the old stories extolling the virtues of Iceland's early settlers and the brave deeds of ancient heroes and gods.

But while Icelanders have won a reputation for being the most fiercely independent and conservative of Scandinavians, they are also, paradoxically, the most enthusiastic members of the Nordic community. An opinion poll commissioned by the Nordic Council in 1983 revealed that Iceland valued Nordic cooperation far more highly than any other Scandinavian country. Unlike Icelanders, the Danes, Finns, Norwegians and Swedes tended to express special interest in individual Nordic countries. However, a majority of people in all five countries were in total agreement about one point: Nordic unity should always take precedence over European ties.

In many ways, the Scandinavian countries today cooperate far more intimately than any other similar union of independent states. Nevertheless, Scandinavia is more aptly described as a family of nations rather than a federation of states. As Patricia Bliss McFate, president of the American Scandinavian Foundation, has observed:

One sometimes hears the phrase "Nordic family." The analogy is helpful not because one can try to pick out the big brother and the naughty little sister, but because it suggests kinship. The countries are a family that grew up together, sharing experiences and beliefs. Now they live apart, but they are siblings. And, although they tease one another, and occasionally quarrel bitterly, they won't fight. □

A LAND OF AWESOME POWER AND INFINITE ENERGY

Iceland is the largest volcanic island in the world, a 40,000-square-mile land mass astride deep fractures in the earth's crust. Most of the geothermal activity occurs in a belt stretching across the island from northeast to southwest. The country's primeval landscape is dramatically scarred with active, snow-capped volcanoes, spouting geysers, hot-water springs, bubbling mud pots and fumaroles (vents emitting hot steam). All testify to the continuing molten ferment deep below Iceland's basalt bedrock.

These forces are now being harnessed to provide one third of Iceland's energy demands. In Reykjavik, the capital, hot water is drawn directly from under the city itself, as well as from neighboring districts, and then stored in huge tanks before being piped to the home radiators of 97 percent of the city's population. For consumers, the use of local energy rather than expensive imported fuel has resulted in savings of up to 25 percent on heating bills. Besides warming homes, subterranean hot water also fills about 30 year-round open-air swimming pools, supplies the breeding tanks of fish hatcheries and heats the country's greenhouses — covering a total of more than 1.5 million square feet — in which are produced fruit, vegetables and flowers.

Such are the benefits of Iceland's immense natural power. At the same time, Icelanders are acutely aware of its destructive potential. On the average, every decade brings two periods of volcanic activity. The most dramatic of recent eruptions came in 1973, when a volcano on the island of Heimaey, less than 10 miles off the south coast of Iceland, destroyed much of the island's only town and forced the evacuation of more than 5,000 people to the mainland. They returned soon after to rebuild their homes and their lives, but the volcano remains a threat.

Sunlight catches a small settlement on the shores of Lake Myvatn in northeast Iceland. The apparent tranquillity of the scene is belied by the nature of the landscape, which incorporates lava terrain, volcanic stumps rising from the water and steam escaping from a field of hot springs in the distant hills.

During one of its spectacular eruptions — which occur roughly every 10 minutes — the geyser known as Stokkur (literally, the "Churn") hurls hot water and steam more than 30 feet into the air. Situated 50 miles northeast of Reykjavik, the spout bursts into life when superheated water is blasted out of the earth.

44

ERUPTIONS FROM SUBTERRANEAN FURNACES

Subterranean steam blows bubbles in a mud pot at Námaskard.

Steam rises from a fumarole at Hveravellir, north of Námaskard.

Shallow terraces formed by successive eruptions of muddy water encircle another steam vent at Hveravellir.

HARNESSING THE FORCES OF NATURE

A pipeline carrying water to cool the drills of the experimental Krafla geothermal power station snakes across a lava landscape in northeast Iceland. In the distance, steam billows from the station's drill holes, which tap subterranean hot springs.

Clouds of steam rise from chimneys of the Sudurnes geothermal plant at Svartsengi in southwest Iceland. The plant is the first in the world to generate power from high-temperature brine, using a complex process to separate energy-producing steam from saline water, which is discarded.

Less than a mile and a half from the Lutheran church on Heimaey Island, a colossal pillar of smoke and ash rises upward from a fissure formed overnight by volcanic action. The flow of molten lava created a hill more than 900 feet high.

In the eruption's aftermath, surviving houses are engulfed in a 13-foot-deep blanket of black tephra — fragments of ash, cinders and pumice ejected by the volcano. Beyond, steam rises from the still-warm lava fields.

Kön. Mayst. in Schweden Gustaui
Adolphi Ankunft in Pommern.
Anno 1630.

Gustavus II, commanding a 13,000-
strong Swedish army, kneels in prayer
before his invasion of Germany in
1630, during the Thirty Years' War. By
the time of his death in battle in 1632,
the king had ensured the survival
of German Protestantism and launched
Sweden as a major European power.

THE NORTHERN SAGA

To the ancient Greeks and Romans, on their warm Mediterranean shores, the Scandinavian world was a cold and mysterious territory, inhabited — in the words of the poet Homer — by "an unhappy race whom endless night invades." The Greek explorer Pythias told tales of a strange, far-off northern isle called Thule, where there was no night at the summer solstice and no day in winter. But the remoteness of this hyperborean region and the rigors of its climate discouraged potential raiders. Indeed, one of the most striking features of the history of Scandinavia is the continuity of settlement by descendants of its earliest inhabitants. By comparison with the rest of Europe, few alien ethnic groups came to conquer or displace the original population. As a result, present-day Scandinavians have a better idea than people in other parts of the world about who their ancestors were and what they looked like.

The bodies of some of these ancestors have been retrieved, almost intact, from the peat bogs of Denmark. Archeologists believe that the best-preserved human head from the Iron Age was found in 1950 at Tollund, in Jutland. Acids in the peat have kept the skin unbroken, the hair intact, the features lifelike and the leather cap almost new — despite its burial roughly 2,000 years ago. The head is now in the Silkeborg Museum in central Jutland where, in the words of a leading authority on bog people, modern Scandinavians curious about their forebears can find themselves "face to face with an Iron Age man."

A large number of finds associated with these early people have enabled archeologists to reconstruct the lifestyle of the early Scandinavians. They lived in village communities or on isolated farmsteads, where they grew barley as a staple crop and raised small herds of sheep and cattle. Their dwellings had walls of turf, floors of clay and roofs of either straw or thatched heather. They stabled their animals at one end of these longhouses to provide themselves with extra warmth in the bitterly cold winters; in addition, they had open hearths on which they made peat-and-wood fires whose smoke rose through a simple hole in the gable. Along the coasts, fishers used nets more than 65 feet long to haul up the riches of the sea. Their boats, some almost 70 feet long, were made of oak and had room for 20 to 30 rowers.

Women wore hand-spun dresses with full skirts and short capes — some of these garments, too, have been found well preserved in the peat bogs. In Copenhagen's National Museum, it is possible to encounter Bronze Age princesses, 500 to 600 years older than Tollund Man. Though their features have been ravaged by time, their gold trinkets still glitter and their amber beads still glow about them.

It was this precious amber — fossilized tree resin, 40 to 60 million years old — that helped bring Scandinavia into contact with the rest of Europe. Centuries before the birth of Christ, pieces of this priceless substance, gathered on the shores of the North Sea and the Baltic, were conveyed slowly to Greece and Rome along a network of overland and river routes. Eventually, Mediterranean mariners made their way north through the Strait of Gibraltar in search of a simpler path to obtain it. Pliny the Elder mentions a Roman sea captain who visited the Baltic coast in about 60 A.D. to buy amber for the Emperor Nero.

The Scandinavian traders who carried the amber south — with furs to adorn the rich Romans and slaves to serve them — returned with Mediterranean gold and luxury goods from the Roman Empire's workshops. Roman vessels of silver and bronze decorated the homes of local chieftains and were buried with them; Roman money and jewels appeared in the households of wealthy traders and farmers. By the second century, the imperial currency had been carried as far north as present-day Finland, where archeologists have unearthed coins minted in the reign of the Emperor Hadrian, who ruled Rome from 117 to 134 A.D.

With the decline and ultimate fall of the empire, in 476 A.D., however, came the epoch of the great migrations that changed the ethnic composition of Europe. Many of the warlike Germanic tribes migrating south and west are thought to have stemmed from Scandinavia, including the Goths from the Baltic coast; the Teutons, a people from the Danish district of Ty; and, from Jutland, the Vandals.

With whole populations on the move and plundering the treasures of the empire, a substantial amount of precious gold gradually found its way

mark and southern Sweden speak of dangerous times, as do the caches of treasure buried nearby. For the most part, they kept to their lands. But late in the eighth century, the Scandinavians burst like lightning on an unsuspecting world. From 800 until the middle of the 11th century, these formerly obscure northerners would be the most powerful force in Western Europe. The Age of the Vikings was about to begin.

Early one spring morning, in 793 A.D., a band of heathen seafarers landed at the holy isle of Lindisfarne, off the coast of northeast England, and launched an attack on the island's wealthy monastery. As one chronicler reported, the raiders "came to the church of Lindisfarne, laid everything waste with grievous plundering, trampled the holy places with polluted feet, dug up the altars and seized all the treasures of the holy church. They killed some of the friars, some they took away in fetters, many they drove out, naked and loaded with insults, and some they drowned in the sea."

Such scenes were repeated innumerable times as all of the neighboring coasts began to feel the keen edge of the Viking sword and battle-ax. The northerners sacked villages and monasteries in England, the Hebrides, Ireland and Wales; they robbed and raped along the coasts of Germany, the Low Countries and northern France. They sailed up the Seine and terrorized the inland settlements, rampaging through Rouen and putting Paris to the torch. Where there was wealth to take, they took it; where there was only poverty, they took slaves instead. And those who resisted, they slaughtered.

The perpetrators of the earliest raids were farmers from Norwegian fjords

north. In Scandinavia itself, the centuries following the Fall of Rome were not merely a turbulent dark age but, as one historian describes it, a "veritable age of gold for the northern barbarians." Scandinavian artisans of the sixth, seventh and eighth centuries produced striking gold decorations and pendants, some of them imitations of Roman coins. Equally impressive were their bronze ornaments, notably brooches of engraved or filigree work depicting strange animals, serpents and intricate, abstract designs.

These people must have been engaged in numerous conflicts among themselves. The remains of fortified earthworks dotting the coasts of Den-

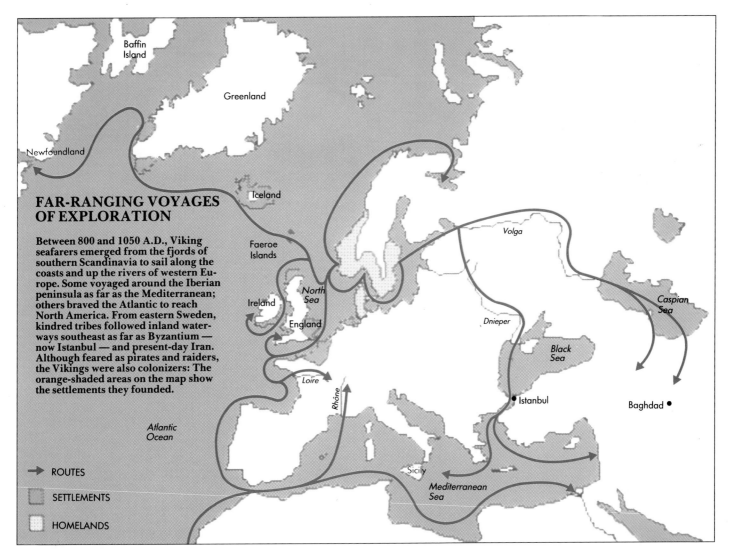

FAR-RANGING VOYAGES OF EXPLORATION

Between 800 and 1050 A.D., Viking seafarers emerged from the fjords of southern Scandinavia to sail along the coasts and up the rivers of western Europe. Some voyaged around the Iberian peninsula as far as the Mediterranean; others braved the Atlantic to reach North America. From eastern Sweden, kindred tribes followed inland waterways southeast as far as Byzantium — now Istanbul — and present-day Iran. Although feared as pirates and raiders, the Vikings were also colonizers: The orange-shaded areas on the map show the settlements they founded.

→ ROUTES

☐ SETTLEMENTS

☐ HOMELANDS

and the coasts of present-day Denmark. In the summer months, between the spring sowing and the autumn harvest, they ventured out on expeditions in quest of riches and honor, leaving the women to run the farms.

These Norsemen called the seasonal forays "going a-viking." The origins of the term are uncertain: It may derive from a word in Old Norse for deep coastal creeks and inlets.

Vikings took pleasure in battle for its own sake and sailed the northern seas in their swift long ships, with high prows, sleek keels, and flexible, seaworthy hulls. In these splendid craft, 80 or 90 men could slip into an alien harbor at night and surprise the sleeping inhabitants by the first light of dawn.

What horses were to the Huns, ships were to the northern marauders. "My mother once told me," reads one of their ancient poems, "she would buy me a long ship, a handsome oared vessel to go sailing with Vikings: To stand at the sternpost and steer a fine warship, then head back for harbor and hew down some foemen."

However, nervous monks and panic-stricken villagers notwithstanding, the

Vikings were not just destroyers. In time they became traders, colonizers, and — from their mastery of the sea — explorers. Short seasonal forays turned into longer expeditions. And for every Norseman who amused himself by wreaking havoc abroad while the crops were growing at home, there was another who set off with his entire family or clan on a peaceable migration.

The Scandinavian homelands — at this time only beginning to emerge as three separate nations — were proving inadequate for the support of an expanding population. Entire families

THE OSEBERG SHIP: TOMB OF A VIKING QUEEN

Covered for a millennium by stone and turf, the Oseberg ship is one of Scandinavia's greatest archeological treasures. The ship, excavated in 1904 at Oseberg farm, near Oslo, was a royal burial place; the grave's contents have made it a valuable source of information about the arts and culture of the early Viking Age.

Historians have suggested that the Oseberg ship may have been the tomb of Queen Asa, who was abducted and forcibly married to Gudrod the Magnificent, a Norwegian ruler. According to legend, she hated Gudrod and had him murdered as he lay in a drunken stupor. She reigned until her death in about 850, when her body was put in a ship brought ashore from Oslo fjord. Archeological evidence indicates that the burial dates from this period.

The ship is clearly the burial place of someone important. Two female skeletons were found, one of them possibly a maid who was sacrificed as part of the funeral ritual. The remains were surrounded by personal possessions — looms, beds and kitchen utensils — which might comfort or serve a queen in the afterlife. Should her ghost wish to travel, the burial ship had sailing gear, including a mast and a full set of 30 oars, as well as four sleighs and an ornately decorated cart.

In a 1904 photograph, the newly excavated Oseberg ship emerges from the burial mound that had covered it for more than 1,000 years.

Fully restored, the Oseberg burial
ship stands in the Viking Ship Museum
in Oslo. Made of oak planking held
together with iron rivets, the ship is
70 feet long, with an elaborately
carved prow and stern soaring 16 feet
above the deck.

Decorations on the wooden cart found
in the ship suggest that the vehicle,
more than 16 feet long, was the possession of a wealthy or royal Viking rather
than a humble farmer. Carvings on the
front depict a man fighting with
snakes — possibly a scene from the life
of Gunnar, a hero of Norse mythology.

2

A detail from an altarpiece in Länna church, in Swedish Uppland, shows Eric IX of Sweden and the English-born Bishop Henry of Uppsala setting sail to convert Finland to Christianity in 1157. Eric became patron saint of Sweden, and Henry — martyred on the mission — patron saint of Finland.

as the result of blood feuds and disputes over property. For those weary of quarrels and revenge — or for those well advised to make themselves scarce — the newly discovered country of Iceland offered a place of refuge. In the middle of the ninth century, Norse sailors, blown off course by storms, had made landfall 560 miles west of Norway, on Iceland's desolate, forbidding coastline, and eventually found their way home, bringing with them tales of virgin territory. When other Vikings began to explore the land with the idea of settling, however, they may have discovered a scattering of Irish monks living as hermits.

By 900, an estimated 15,000 to 20,000 people, emigrating from mainland Norway and the Norse colonies in Ireland, had settled in Iceland. They were led by 38 chieftains who brought with them their entire households, including families and tenants, retainers and thralls (slaves). About the year 930, the heads of these first families of Iceland established the Althing, a lawmaking council of elders that evolved into a parliament and has functioned almost without interruption ever since; an institution by the same name still exists as the government of the present-day Republic of Iceland.

The Icelanders, during the long winter nights, became a nation of storytellers, recording the great events of their day in the prose narratives known as sagas. Originating from the 11th century onward, and passed down orally by generations of long-memoried bards, these tales paint a richly detailed picture of Viking life: blood feuds, domestic dramas of the kitchen and the farmyard, foolhardy exploits and the adventurous voyages of discovery.

The rest of Europe marveled at the

took to the sea in search of more hospitable territory. The Danes peacefully colonized many coastal areas of eastern England, where hundreds of Danish place names remain today as records of their settlement. The Norwegians were chronically short of arable land; therefore, they emigrated to the Orkneys, the Shetlands, the Faeroes, and the Hebrides, as well as to parts of Ireland,

northwest England and Scotland. They made their homes in the Frisian Islands in the North Sea, along the Dutch and Belgian river estuaries, and on the French coasts near the mouth of the River Seine — a region that came to be known as Normandy after the French kings formally ceded it to a group of Norse settlers in 911.

Other Scandinavians left their homes

stories it heard about Iceland's natural wonders. "Here there is a strange spring from whose water there rises a fuming stench which changes all it touches to stone though it keeps its first form and shape," reported the 12th-century Danish historian Saxo Grammaticus. "There are also here many wells and streams which from time to time overflow their waters and shoot them high into the air, spraying with white foam all that is near at hand." He continued, "On this same island there is the mountain of Hekla, which forever burns and flames. It is a wonder that the mountain, which is covered on all sides with ice and snow, can nevertheless find enough fuel for its continuous and unquenching fire." Perhaps most surprising of all, "there are also springs in which the water tastes of beer."

One of the settlers on this remarkable island, Eric the Red, was banished from Iceland for three years by a local court after a blood feud with a neighbor. Spurred on by sailors' tales of an enormous land mass lying far to the west, he and a small band of followers set forth from Iceland in the summer of 982, sailed due west for almost 200 miles and landed in Greenland, populated only by roving Eskimos. During the years of his exile, Eric explored the glaciers, fjords and arctic meadows of the new-found country. When his term of banishment ended, he returned to Iceland, gathered up a band of potential settlers and led them back to Greenland in 986. Encouraged by Eric, they established a colony on the coastlands of its southwestern tip, along fjords that were teeming with fish.

In the year 1000, Eric's son, Leif Ericson, alias Leif the Lucky, sailed even farther west and discovered a land he

Depicted in a 1510 hymnal, Saint Bridget of Sweden receives the rules of a new monastic order from Jesus and Mary. Bridget, a visionary who died in 1373, was concerned with world events as well as theology, advising the pope on European politics and proposing a plan to end the Hundred Years' War.

57

called Vinland — according to his saga — "because vines producing excellent wine grow wild there; moreover, self-sown wheat grows there in abundance." He and his crew had discovered America, five centuries before Columbus. Although the place where they landed has yet to be identified, archeologists have unearthed Viking remains farther north, well beyond the grape-growing area, at the northernmost tip of Newfoundland.

The Vikings were too few in number, however, to maintain themselves in North America. Even the Greenland colony, which grew to an estimated 3,000 to 5,000 settlers, eventually lost contact with Europe. When Norwegian explorers returned, late in the 17th century, there was no longer any sign of people other than the native Eskimos. The fate of the settlers remains a mystery: They may have been defeated by a rapidly deteriorating climate or they may have been absorbed by the Eskimo population. Another possibility, suggested by an Eskimo oral tradition, was that there may have been quarrels during which the Norwegian population was annihilated.

Throughout the Viking age, while the Norwegians and Danes had looked westward to the Atlantic, Swedish adventurers — known as the Varangians — turned their attentions eastward, to the lands across the Baltic Sea. They traveled south from Lake Ladoga and over the watershed to the Volga, the Don and the Dnieper in order to trade iron, furs and slaves for Saracen silver and gold. Some stopped to establish local kingdoms, first at Novgorod, within easy reach of the Baltic Sea, then at Kiev, two thirds of the way to the Black Sea. The indigenous population called the interlopers Rus, possibly

from an early word for "horse" — which eventually led to the whole country being called Russia.

During the summer of 921, one Ibn Fadlan, an emissary of the caliph at Baghdad, encountered a group of Vikings who were encamped along the shores of the Volga. He stayed with them long enough to write a lengthy, detailed description of them as a kind of intelligence report for his government. Since Ibn Fadlan was an educated man, schooled in the courtly customs of one of the world's most fastidious civilizations, he was rather taken aback by the manners of these incredibly bumptious barbarians. What makes his report all the more fascinating is that it constitutes the only extant account of life among the Vikings when they were not raiding and plundering as well as the only description of the Vikings as seen through the eyes of a neutral observer. "I saw the Rus who were there for commerce and come down the River Atul [Volga]," he wrote. "I have never seen bodies more perfect than theirs. One would say they are as tall as palm trees"; and all were armed with "an ax, sword and knife.

"They are the filthiest people under

God. They never wash off excrement or urine; they do not wash after sexual relations, they do not wash their hands after meals. They are like wild donkeys." They also brought with them "beautiful young female slaves intended for the slave merchants."

Elsewhere in Europe, however, there were powerful civilizing forces at work among the Scandinavian immigrants. The early Vikings had been pagans, untouched by the missionary monks who had brought the Christian faith to the rest of Western Europe several centuries before. But, as early as the ninth century, some of the Norwegians who settled among the Franks were converted to Christianity. The Danish chieftains who established the occupied territory known as the Danelaw in north and east England soon were baptized and were permitted burial in Christian churches. Olaf Sitricson (Olaf the Red), the ruler of Dublin from 941 to 980, also became a Christian. Finally, toward the end of the 10th century, the kings of Denmark, Norway and Sweden were converted to the new faith, after years of patient efforts by missionary monks. Their subjects rapidly followed the kings into the Christian faith, some-

An executioner dispatches a Swedish noble while two churchmen are hustled toward the block in a contemporary etching of the 1520 Stockholm Bloodbath. Christian II of Denmark ordered the massacre of his opponents to ensure his ascendancy.

times persuaded by sermons, sometimes by swords. The Icelandic Althing agreed to accept Christianity about the year 1000 — though with due allowance for the continuation of some of the traditional pagan practices.

It was not a difficult shift for most people: In place of the cruciform amulet known as Thor's hammer, which they had always worn around their necks, they now wore the symbol of Christ's Cross. The names for most of the days of the week remained the same, still consecrated to the pagan gods: Tiu's day, of the god of war and the sky; Wodin's day, of the one-eyed chief of the gods; Thor's day, dedicated to the god of Thunder; and Frigg's day, which belonged to Wodin's wife, the goddess of the heavens.

By the 11th century, Scandinavia was dotted with Christian churches, many of them built on the sites of the old pagan burial mounds and holy places. Though the new creed did not prevent them from making war on their neighbors, the Scandinavian kings were now Christian monarchs and therefore subject to the moral restraints of the medieval Church. Monastic foundations multiplied; traveling architects from Germany, France, Italy and England came to construct stone churches; nunneries and hospitals were founded; and the Scandinavian faithful pilgrimaged along routes still trodden today to their first shrine — that dedicated to Saint Olaf in Trondheim.

Increasingly, Christian monarchs such as Harold Bluetooth of Denmark and Knud II (Canute the Great) treated the Church as the one institution that could bring unity, discipline and prosperity to their strife-torn dominions. Its teachings reinforced their authority: In the orderly Christian hierarchy, the king rules over his subjects, but God rules over the king.

It was Knud who gave his courtiers the famous object lesson of placing his throne at the water's edge at low tide and bidding the sea "not to rise over my land, and not to presume to wet the clothes and limbs of your lord." Then, after the disobedient waves had wetted his feet, the king jumped back on dry land and told his retainers: "Be it known to all inhabitants of the world that the power of kings is empty and superficial, and that no one is worthy of the name of king except for Him whose will is obeyed by heaven, earth and sea in accordance with eternal laws."

In the year 1066, King Harald III (Harold Hard-Ruler) of Norway made one last attempt to invade England in

order to wrest the crown from its newly proclaimed king, Harold II (son of the Earl of Wessex), who was himself the grandson of a Viking raider. Harald III was killed in action near York, and his army was thrown back into the sea. But only three weeks later, at the Battle of Hastings, Harold II himself was killed and his army was routed by 10,000 men led by William II, Duke of Normandy, another invader who had Viking blood running in his veins.

William subsequently took systematic measures to protect his new realm from attacks by Norway or Denmark, securing the coast with a chain of well-armed fortresses. Never again was England threatened by a large-scale Scandinavian invasion.

The following centuries of Scandinavian history were marked by political concerns much closer to home. The annals of the late Middle Ages tell of shifting rivalries and alliances in a three-sided struggle for power among the kings of Denmark, Norway and Sweden and of frequent warfare against hostile neighbors.

At the same time, the Scandinavian climate was becoming markedly colder; by the late 1300s, northern Europe was entering a little ice age that was to continue for the next 400 years. With deteriorating climatic conditions, crops repeatedly failing and animals suffering correspondingly, the population throughout the Scandinavian world went into a decline. Iceland, according to the tax records of 1096, had only 50,000 inhabitants, and the island's population probably remained at that level for several centuries.

Many previously cultivated areas were abandoned, and the overall area of settlement contracted as famine and pestilence overtook communities, in-

The sandy beard and aggressive stance of Gustavus I, known as Gustavus Vasa, are captured by contemporary artist Willem Boy. Vasa was elected king by the Swedish nobility in 1523, after he led a revolt against the Danes.

A CHRONOLOGY OF KEY EVENTS

c. 8,000 B.C. As the Ice Age wanes, the earliest migrants enter Scandinavia, living first by hunting and fishing, then by limited agriculture and herding. Settlement is sparse, lagging far behind more southerly regions.

c. 2,000 B.C. New peoples — probably direct ancestors of today's inhabitants — move northward into Scandinavia, introducing the use of the ax. Settlement spreads into the forests. Trade develops with the rest of Europe.

1,500-500 B.C. A thriving Bronze Age civilization develops, linked by trade with Mediterranean cultures. Archeological finds from this period include woolen textiles, gold, jewelry, amber and the bronze horns known as *lurs (above)*.

450-500 A.D. During the dissolution of the western Roman Empire, Scandinavia remains outside most of the disturbances, but it is enriched by plunder that is circulating in barbarian possession. Local warfare occupies the small kingships and loose tribal groupings of the nascent Scandinavian nations.

800-1050 Impelled by overpopulation at home, Viking crews embark on raiding and trading expeditions that ultimately affect most of the Western world. Vikings from Sweden reach Byzantium though Russia; western Vikings from Denmark and Norway plunder and settle European seacoasts and Iceland.

874 Norsemen colonize Iceland.

c. 930 Icelandic settlers form a commonwealth, initiating 300 years of self-government.

986 Settlers from Iceland colonize Greenland.

c. 1000 Leif Ericsson leaves Iceland and reaches North America. Christianity is adopted by the Icelandic commonwealth, and by the kings of Norway, Denmark and Sweden.

1017 Canute the Great (Knud II), later king of Denmark, defeats an English army and becomes king of England.

1120-1230 The sagas — prose tales of Norse history and legend — are composed in Iceland.

1262 Weakened by economic hardship and internal feuding, Iceland and Greenland come under the rule of the king of Norway.

1293 Finland is conquered and annexed by Sweden.

c. 1350 The Black Death reaches Scandinavia, reducing the population by as much as two thirds in some areas.

1397 Denmark, Norway (with Iceland) and Sweden (with Finland) come under one rule when Denmark's Queen Margrete creates the Union of Kalmar and crowns her great-nephew, Eric of Pomerania, king of the three realms.

1477 The first Scandinavian university is founded at Uppsala in Sweden, followed two years later by the University of Copenhagen in Denmark.

1520 In an attempt to quell Swedish resistance to Danish control, King Christian II of Denmark *(below)* has his opponents murdered in Stockholm.

1523 In reaction to King Christian's tyranny, Sweden revolts from union with Denmark-Norway.

1527 Gustavus I establishes the Lutheran Church in Sweden and Finland. Ten years later, Denmark, together with Norway and Iceland, adopts Lutheranism.

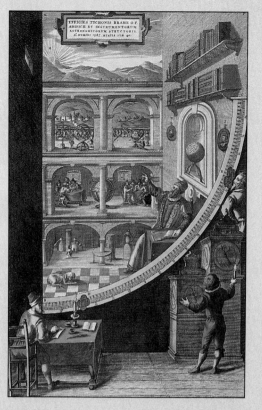

1539 The Swedish priest Olaus Magnus publishes a pictorial map of Scandinavia, followed by a history of the Scandinavian peoples in 1555, giving the rest of Europe its first visual and textual documentation on the lands and culture of the North.

1563-1570 Denmark-Norway defeats Sweden in the Scandinavian Seven Years' War.

1573 The Danish astronomer Tycho Brahe publishes his great work, *De Nova Stella*. With the patronage of King Frederik II, Brahe sets up an observatory *(above)*, where he works for 20 years improving the accuracy of astronomical observations.

1602 Denmark declares trade monopoly over Iceland.

1611-1613 The Kalmar War, another conflict between Denmark-Norway and Sweden, ends with a treaty marking the start of a period of economic and territorial expansion for Sweden. The nation advances to create a Baltic empire at the expense of Poland and Russia.

1611-1632 Reign of Gustavus II. Sweden plays a major part in the Thirty Years' War.

1638 Sweden establishes a colony in America: Fort Christina on the Delaware River.

1640 A university is founded at Abo in Finland.

1654 Queen Christina of Sweden abdicates after a 22-year reign and becomes a Roman Catholic. Her cousin Charles X becomes king.

1697-1721 Charles XII of Sweden undertakes overambitious campaigns against Denmark, Poland, Saxony and Russia, and is killed in battle in 1718. Sweden subsequently loses its powerful position and much of its trans-Baltic territory.

1735 The Swedish naturalist Linnaeus publishes his *Systema Naturae,* the foundation for naming and classifying plant and animal species.

1807 British forces bombard Copenhagen, driving Denmark into an alliance with Napoleonic France.

1809 Sweden is forced to cede Finland to Russia; the country becomes a Russian grand duchy with limited self-government.

1810 The Swedish Parliament elects one of Napoleon's field marshals — Bernadotte — as heir to the childless Charles XIII. The new crown prince takes the title Karl Johan *(below).*

1814 In spite of Norwegian reluctance, Karl Johan secures Norway's separation from Denmark. Although ruled by the king of Sweden, Norway remains a separate state and retains its own constitution.

1825 The first Norwegian emigrant ship sails to America.

1835-1850 A growing interest in indigenous Scandinavian culture is marked by the publication of Elias Lönnrot's *Kalevala* — a compilation of Finnish folk epics — and the Norwegian folk tales collected by P.C. Asbjörnsen and Jørgen Moe. The folk form is elaborated by the Dane Hans Christian Andersen in his fairy tales.

1844 The first of Denmark's folk high schools brings political and cultural education to rural children.

1864 Denmark, defeated in war by Prussia and Austria, loses the duchies of Schleswig and Holstein — about one third of its territory.

1860-1900 A cultural flowering, or northern renaissance, brings to prominence the writers Ibsen and Strindberg, the painter Munch and the composers Grieg and Sibelius.

1878-1880 The Finnish explorer A. E. Nordenskjöld takes the first ship through the Arctic via the Northeast Passage across the top of Asia.

1888 The Norwegian explorer Fridtjof Nansen makes the first crossing of Greenland, then goes on to make other polar expeditions.

1905 The union of Norway and Sweden is dissolved. Prince Carl of Denmark is elected ruler of an independent Norway, with the title of King Haakon VII.

1906 After a period of repression and resistance, Russia permits the establishment of a Finnish parliament. Universal suffrage makes Finland the first European nation to give women the vote. Norway soon follows.

1911-1912 Roald Amundsen, a Norwegian, leads the first successful expedition to the South Pole.

1914-1918 The three Scandinavian kingdoms remain neutral during World War I.

1918 Civil war follows Finland's declaration of independence from Russia in December 1917. After leading a volunteer army to victory, General Carl Gustaf Mannerheim becomes regent of an independent Finland.

1918 Iceland becomes independent under a Danish-Icelandic monarchy.

1925 The Swedish star Greta Garbo *(above, right)* makes her movie debut.

1933-1936 Sweden institutes social security programs. Denmark introduces public works projects for unemployment relief. Norway sets up state pensions and unemployment insurance.

1939-1940 At the outset of World War II, Denmark and Norway are occupied by Germany. Iceland is occupied by the Western allies. Finland goes to war with the Soviet Union, while Sweden stays neutral.

1944 Iceland declares independence from Denmark.

1948 After Finland undertakes to pay war reparations to the Soviet Union, the two nations sign the Treaty of Friendship, Cooperation and Mutual Assistance.

1949 Norway, Denmark and Iceland join NATO.

1952 Denmark, Norway, Iceland and Sweden form the Nordic Council for economic, social and cultural cooperation. Finland joins the council three years later.

1958 Iceland and Britain clash over fishing rights in the first "Cod War." Hostilities finally end in 1976 when Britain accedes to Iceland's 200-mile fishing limit.

1980 Iceland elects the world's first woman president, Vigdis Finnbogadottir. In Sweden, failed wage negotiations create the worst labor dispute in the nation's history, with 25 percent of the work force on strike or locked out.

1981 Norway puts into production recently discovered reserves of North Sea oil and gas, giving it some protection from the worldwide recession affecting the other Nordic countries.

1986 Swedish Prime Minister Olof Palme is gunned down by a lone assassin on Stockholm's main thoroughfare, shocking the peace-loving Swedes. It is the first murder of a Swedish leader in almost 200 years, since Gustavus III was shot to death at a masked ball in 1792.

2

spiring the *Dance of Death* paintings that still decorate medieval Scandinavian church walls. In these grotesque reminders of mortality, a grinning Grim Reaper leads his victims in a dance: young and old; rich and poor; king, priest and peasant alike; all forced to tread his measure. This was the time of the Black Death — bubonic plague, carried by ship around the coasts of Europe — which devastated much of Scandinavia. In some parts of Norway, two thirds of the populace was annihilated in a matter of months.

It was during this tumultuous era that Finland was drawn into the Scandinavian sphere. Living in small communities along the coasts, beside the island-dotted lakes or along the banks of fast-flowing rivers, the Finns were peasant farmers, hunters, fishers and modest fur traders. Ruled by no king and defended by no army, they were a prime target for invaders.

Between the 11th and the 14th centuries, Swedish armies marched into Finland for missionary as well as military reasons. With the blessing of the pope in Rome, Swedish crusaders converted Finland's pagan population to Christianity and began a process of political and cultural domination that lasted until the 19th century.

These crusades were motivated, at least in part, by the need to fend off dangerous influences from the East: missionaries from Russia who were entering Finland and spreading the Eastern Orthodox version of the Christian faith, a spiritual as well as a secular threat to the power of the Roman Catholic Church. As they advanced, the Swedish invaders consolidated their position by constructing a line of fortresses at strategic points along the southern coasts of Finland.

Under the influence of their Swedish conquerors, the Finns were drawn into the emerging culture of the Renaissance. Before the first Scandinavian universities were founded — at Uppsala in 1477 and in Copenhagen in 1479 — Finnish and Swedish students regularly made their way to Paris, where some of them obtained master's degrees, or attended German universities, returning to their own lands with the fruits of the new humanist movements in science and the arts.

But German influence, in particular, extended beyond cultural exchange. During the 14th century, most of Scandinavia's growing maritime trade was controlled by the powerful association of German merchants known as the Hanseatic League, which managed to impose its will on the kings of Denmark, Norway and Sweden by force of arms. The league was multinational, comprising 70 member cities that stretched from Nantes to Novgorod. It dominated Baltic commerce from Lübeck, the richest of all the Hanse towns, and established German trading enclaves in the principal Scandinavian commercial centers, such as Bergen's Tyskebryggen — the German Quay — lined with the well-filled warehouses of the league. In some of the Gothic churches built by the Hanseatic merchants, services were to be conducted in German for several hundred years.

The concluding years of the 14th century brought with them a turning point in Nordic history — the Union of Three Crowns, sometimes called the Union of Kalmar, under Queen Margrete in 1397. Margrete, a daughter of the King of Denmark, married the King of Norway and became regent of both countries following the death of her husband and her son, the infant

A 17th-century painting shows a red carpet stretching from Copenhagen Castle to the dais where Frederik III, illuminated by a shaft of sunlight, is being declared Denmark's first absolute and hereditary king. On the far left is the artist, deaf-mute Wolfgang Heimbach, waving his hat.

2

Danish king. By dint of shrewd diplomacy — and a disputed family claim to the Swedish crown — she soon persuaded the Swedes, too, to accept her as Sovereign Lady and Ruler. To weld the three kingdoms together, Margrete arranged for her infant kinsman, Eric VII of Pomerania, to be crowned king of Denmark, Norway and Sweden. Under his rule, the three states retained their own laws and customs and were administered by their own dignitaries: It was a union of crowns rather than kingdoms that was to last — despite internal dissensions and a period of secession by the disgruntled Swedes — for more than 100 years.

The Union of Three Crowns was finally brought to an end in the early 1500s through the misuse of royal authority by King Christian II. Determined to break the power of the nobles, Christian attempted to turn the merchant class against the landed aristocracy. But in Sweden, he met with resistance from all sectors of the population, and the Swedish delegates to the assembly of notables that gathered in Copenhagen in 1513 flatly refused to recognize Christian as their king. "We have," they declared, "the choice between peace at home and strife here, or peace here and civil war at home, and we prefer the former."

Christian immediately launched a series of campaigns intended to bring Sweden to heel, but not until 1520 did he succeed in occupying the city of Stockholm and compelling the resident nobles to recognize his sovereignty. Then, after three days of banqueting, he gave a signal to a troop of Danish soldiers and they arrested the guests — his former adversaries. Scores of Swedish leaders, including nobles, bishops,

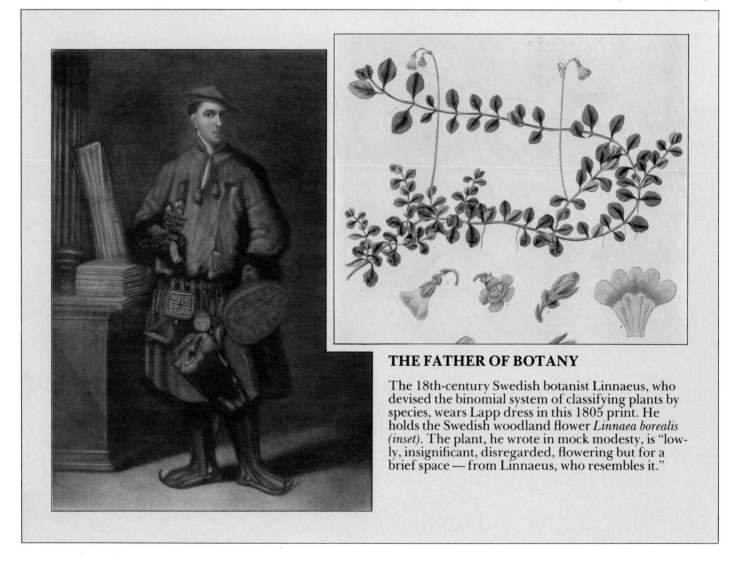

THE FATHER OF BOTANY

The 18th-century Swedish botanist Linnaeus, who devised the binomial system of classifying plants by species, wears Lapp dress in this 1805 print. He holds the Swedish woodland flower *Linnaea borealis (inset)*. The plant, he wrote in mock modesty, is "lowly, insignificant, disregarded, flowering but for a brief space — from Linnaeus, who resembles it."

burgomasters and town councilors, were later beheaded or drowned in what came to be known as the Stockholm Bloodbath. In all, about 600 people were slaughtered, and the corpses of opponents already buried were exhumed so that they could be burned on a pyre with the rest. Later, Christian explained his policies by declaring, "Mild measures are of no use; the remedies that give the whole body a good shaking are the best and surest."

The king's tyrannies produced the inevitable backlash: Sweden rose in revolt, and when Christian attempted to coerce Denmark and Norway into a war against the rebellious kingdom, they too renounced their allegiance and offered the Danish-Norwegian crown to Christian's uncle, Frederik I (Duke of Holstein). Eventually, Christian was forced to surrender to his rival, and for the last 27 years of his life he was kept in solitary confinement.

After the collapse of the union, Denmark and Norway remained together as a single realm, a relationship that would last until 1814.

In Sweden, after the Stockholm massacre and Christian's downfall, a new king — Gustavus I, or Gustavus Vasa — was elected by an assembly representing the nobles, clergy and commoners of the realm. Gustavus' reign opened an irreparable breach with the Vatican: His father had been murdered on the orders of the bishop of Stockholm, an adviser to the deposed tyrant Christian, and an implacable enmity grew up between the papacy and the new regime.

Although Gustavus I held no strong theological opinions, the rift caused him to side with Germany's Lutherans. Within a decade, the newly independent Swedish nation had become one of the great strongholds of Protestantism,

and Finland — as the eastern wing of Sweden — followed suit.

In the 16th century, Sweden and Denmark-Norway established themselves as formidable naval powers. Denmark controlled the entrance to the Baltic, collecting tolls at the strategically sited Kronborg Castle, at Helsingor — the Elsinore of Shakespeare's *Hamlet* — where the Oresund is at its narrowest. Standing guard over these straits, the Danes levied tribute on foreign shipping until 1857.

Sweden, on the other hand, enjoyed a monopoly of such naval stores as pitch and Stockholm tar; in an age of wooden ships, no European merchant fleets or navies could survive without these essential materials, used for waterproof-

ing their vessels. Sweden was also Europe's main source of the pig iron and copper ingots used for the manufacture of bronze cannon and other military hardware.

As the rival states grew in strength, their contest for the domination of the Baltic intensified. In a bid to acquire new domains on the eastern shore of the sea, Sweden became embroiled in the affairs of Poland and Russia, fighting now on one side, now on the other, in accordance with shifts in the balance of power. But, for the time being, Denmark held sovereignty on the seas. So powerful was Denmark's fleet during the latter half of the 16th century that Frederick II was able to enforce a rule that all foreign ships were to strike

2

their topsails whenever they met a Danish man-of-war.

Twice the competing nations measured their strength on the battlefield. In the Scandinavian Seven Years' War, from 1563 to 1570, and in the Kalmar War from 1611 to 1613 (so called after the hotly contended fortress of that name), Denmark-Norway emerged the victor on both occasions. But the second of these conflicts ended with a treaty that brought peace for a time to the nations. Each rival returned the territories it had conquered, though Sweden was compelled to pay the Danes a massive indemnity.

The Swedish King Gustavus II, also called Gustavus Adolphus, whose reign began at the start of the Kalmar War, was to play a key role in the subsequent era of expansion. During his 21-year reign, from 1611 to 1632, Sweden became virtually an empire, as displayed in the magnificent baroque maps of his realm, which were drawn for him at this time. The kingdom now entered into a golden age of increased prosperity at home and prestige abroad that would last for the rest of the 17th century.

Sweden's growing might derived not only from the kingdom's natural resources but also from the fact that it was one of the most efficient European states of the day. Important factors in its political success were its military and naval competence, its governmental organization and its adoption of the latest technological innovations.

Accordingly, Gustavus Adolphus was destined to become one of the few successful Protestant generals of the Thirty Years' War that devastated central Europe between 1618 and 1648. In 1630, he led an army of 16,000 Swedes into Germany to deliver the Lutherans from tyranny. Within months he had defeated the far more powerful forces of the Hapsburg Emperor Ferdinand II and had made himself master of Germany from Saxony to the Rhine. After two years of campaigning, however, Gustavus was killed on the battlefield of Lützen, just as he was about to win another hard-fought victory. His heart was sent home to Sweden, wrapped in a silken shirt.

Gustavus Adolphus was 37 years old when he died; his only child, daughter of a Prussian princess, was six years old at the time. Princess Christina grew up to be a gifted but also headstrong and extravagant queen. "Her majesty is not like womenfolk," declared her chief minister, Axel Oxenstierna, when she was only 15, "but is stouthearted and of good understanding so that, if she be not corrupted, we have good hopes for her."

When she succeeded to the throne in her 18th year (the silver throne made for her coronation is still used by the king of Sweden when he opens the Swedish Parliament), Christina did her best to bring the Thirty Years' War to an end — if only because peace would allow her to jettison the officious and overbearing Oxenstierna. At home, she ruled with a lavish but energetic hand, encouraging trade and manufacturing and ennobling members of the middle class. Abroad, her sea captains attempted to plant the seeds of an American empire: Swedish and Dutch settlers established Fort Christina at the mouth of the Delaware River, where the city of Wilmington is today.

But in her late twenties, Christina grew weary of affairs of state and rebelled at the idea of submitting to the will of her cousin, who was chosen to become her husband. Instead of marrying him, she designated him her successor — Charles X Gustavus — and, in 1654, performed the solemn act of abdication, in which she placed her own crown on Charles's head.

Still feted as queen, Christina journeyed to Rome, converted to Catholicism with pomp and circumstance and then proceeded to scandalize the pope and Roman aristocracy with her hedonistic lifestyle. She lived lavishly in the Farnese Palace on a Swedish state pension, collecting art and exploring antiquities by day and giving notoriously debauched parties by night.

By the middle of the 17th century, Sweden had emerged as a major military power. It was then one of the largest states of Europe, with about twice as much territory as it has today. A great part of this land had been acquired from Denmark-Norway, whose power was fast receding: It was not until the 18th century that the pendulum swung back again, so that a certain equilibrium was reestablished between the Danes and the Swedes.

Ironically, one of the boldest, most ambitious of Sweden's rulers presided over the empire's downfall. Charles XII, in his military moves against Denmark, Poland, Saxony and Russia, fatally overextended the human and financial resources of his kingdom. After his death in battle in 1718, his demoralized armies returned, and Sweden was forced to surrender to Russia much of the Baltic territory it had acquired in the years of imperial expansion.

As the empire fell, the threat from the east grew greater. The Swedish Grand Duchy of Finland was devastated by what came to be called the Great Wrath — a seven-year period of occupation by Russian troops that ended in 1721. The Northern War that

preceded it had already cost Finland most of her young men, and the harshness of the occupation, coupled with widespread crop failure, drove one quarter of the country people from their farms and reduced the population from about 400,000 to fewer than 300,000. One document of the era reads that, in marking the passing of those who died of hunger, "church bells tolled until they cracked." From that time, Swedish power in Finland was to be increasingly threatened by the growing military and economic might of the Russian tsars.

The pressure on Sweden's eastern flank led to one of the nation's most significant administrative achievements: the first modern census. In 1750, partly motivated by a need to an-ticipate labor and food resources in case of war, data was collected from every parish, monitoring births, marriages, deaths, causes of mortality and the movements of the population.

Even without the exigencies of national security, the gathering of information was a major passion of the age. In this century of intellectual enlightenment, Swedish science was spurred on by such figures as Linnaeus, the brilliant naturalist, who systematized the study of botany, and Anders Celsius, the astronomer, who invented the centigrade thermometer.

At the same time, the Swedish aristocracy acquired new polish and sophistication as patrons of art and letters. Under their sponsorship, Swedish literature and scholarship flourished.

Commissioned by wealthy nobles, local and foreign architects produced a succession of baroque and rococo masterpieces. One of the nation's finest palaces was built during this era, Drottningholm, on the shore of Lake Malar near Stockholm. This architectural gem, incorporating formal gardens, a court theater and a Chinese summer house, was Scandinavia's answer to Versailles, a gathering place for the most glittering artistic, intellectual and musical talents of the day.

The moving spirit behind this lively court was King Gustavus III (1746-1792), who founded the Swedish Academy, built the first theater and opera house in Stockholm and was himself a famous playwright. The king's career was cut short, however, when he was assassinated at a masked ball held in March 1792, at his own opera house. The murder was the work of a group of disaffected nobles vainly hoping to regain their eroded powers. Gustavus had been warned of the plot beforehand, but stubbornly refused to cancel his engagement. (Half a century later, Giuseppe Verdi composed his opera *Un Ballo in Maschera* to a libretto linked with this incident.)

The assassination of Gustavus anticipated the end of an era — the demise of absolutist monarchy in Scandinavia. For more than a century, both Sweden and Denmark-Norway had been ruled by autocratic sovereigns who professed to derive their authority from "the divine right of kings." Even the isolated, self-reliant Icelanders, whose trade had been subjected to total monopoly by the Danes, suffered from the increasing whims and decrees of the kings of Denmark. However, not all Danish monarchs abused their power. Christian VI, who ruled from 1730 to 1746, was praised by his contemporary, the great Danish playwright Ludvig Holberg, for "a reign of bliss when everything seemed to gain new life and energies."

But by the end of the 18th century, absolutism had clearly run its course. The French Revolution demonstrated to the rest of Europe how easy it was to depose and decapitate a king. But France rapidly found itself in the grip of a no-less-inexorable absolutist, Napoleon Bonaparte, who was soon at war with most of Europe in his campaign to maintain his power.

Both Sweden and Denmark-Norway were drawn into the maelstrom of the Napoleonic wars, though on opposite sides. Denmark-Norway endeavored to remain neutral in the bitter conflict between Britain and France, but the British navy twice intervened in order to prevent the Danish fleet from falling into French hands and to maintain open access to Scandinavia's supply of essential naval stores. In 1801, a British expeditionary force under the command of Admiral Horatio Nelson landed in Denmark and seized almost the entire Danish fleet. In retaliation, Denmark made common cause with Napoleon and remained his ally until his defeat at the Battle of Leipzig in 1813.

Sweden, in the meantime, found itself at war against Russia, France and Denmark-Norway. In 1808, Russian troops invaded Finland and occupied the whole of the grand duchy. In the wake of this defeat, the young and inept Swedish King Gustavus IV was deposed and replaced by his elderly uncle, Charles XIII. It was King Charles who acceded to the 1809 Treaty of Frederikshamn, which yielded the Grand Duchy of Finland to Russia — from that time, Tsar Alexander I of Russia would wear a second crown, as Grand Duke of Finland.

Since Charles was only an interim king, childless and infirm, the Swedish Parliament made repeated attempts to find a candidate for the succession. The choice fell on one of Napoleon's most capable — and disaffected — field marshals, Jean Baptiste Bernadotte, who was popular in Stockholm because of the kindness he had shown toward the Swedish prisoners in the war with Denmark. Soon after his arrival in the Swedish capital in 1810, he was elected crown prince and formally adopted as a son by the elderly, failing king. He chose to be called Karl Johan.

During the final years of the Napoleonic wars, Karl Johan — whose relations with Napoleon had always been stormy — turned against his former chief to command the Swedish army in the field. In 1813, he headed the northern front in the critical campaign that led to Bonaparte's defeat at Leipzig. Within a year, he had also achieved his principal ambition — that of separating Norway from Denmark and attaching it instead to Sweden.

Denmark — defeated in war and officially bankrupt — had no choice but to consent to the new arrangement. To some extent, the Danes were compensated for their loss by receiving Swedish Pomerania, on the southern coast of the Baltic Sea; they were also permitted to retain the old Norse colonies of Iceland, Greenland and the Faeroe Islands. The Norwegians, however, had not been consulted, and they acknowledged their new rulers only after Karl Johan invaded their country with Swedish troops in 1814. In the ensuing compromise, Norway was proclaimed "a free, independent and indivisible kingdom united with Sweden under one king." It was accorded its own constitution and the right to elect its own parliament, the Storting, with freedom to legislate internal affairs with little interference from the Swedish crown.

Partly in response to these political developments, the people of Norway and Finland began to assert their national identities. Inspired by nationalism, the Norwegians and Finns set about rediscovering their literary past and codifying their written languages. In Norway, the folklorists Asbjörnsen and Moe began to collect the old rural tales and legends; and the Romantic canvases of artist J. C. Dahl captured the rugged grandeur of the Norwegian landscape. In the meantime, the official Danish language of administration and the courts, Riksmål, now known as Bokmål, was complemented by the vernacular of the Norwegian country people — Landsmål, or Nynorsk, as it has come to be called.

In Finland, long under foreign linguistic as well as political domination, the national revival of the native language — and the creation of written Finnish — was given impetus in 1835 by the first publication of *Kalevala*. This collection of ancient folk poetry had been passed down orally through generations of storytellers and put together by the apothecary Elias Lönnrot. Finnish, which had been recognized as an official language jointly with Swedish and Russian in 1860, eventually became a central feature in the struggle against Russian rule. But while the Finnish language fostered a new sense of nationhood, it also opened a serious split between the Finnish-speaking majority and the Swedish-speaking minority within the grand duchy.

Elsewhere in Europe, the 19th century ushered in an epoch of big-power politics, and the Scandinavian nations were forced to adjust to a considerably diminished role: After some 300 years as military and diplomatic powers to be reckoned with, Sweden and Denmark now found themselves buffeted by international events they could no longer influence or control. Denmark, for example, lost about a third of its territory when Prussia's "Iron Chancellor," Otto von Bismarck, initiated a brief war between Prussia and Denmark in 1864. Hostilities ended with Germany annexing Slesvig (Schleswig) and Holstein, two duchies that had formed part of the Danish monarchy for 500 years.

But what 19th-century Denmark lost in temporal power, it more than made up in intellectual prestige — thanks to scientists such as H. C. Ørsted, writers such as Søren Kierkegaard and Hans Christian Andersen, and artists such as the sculptor Bertel Thorvaldsen. This northern renaissance also extended to the rest of Scandinavia: The Norwegian playwright Henrik Ibsen and the Swedish author August Strindberg revolutionized European ideas of theater just as the Norwegian painter Edvard Munch helped launch the Expressionist movement in art, and composers such as Jean Sibelius in Finland and Carl Nielsen in Denmark extended the range of symphonic music.

Despite this creative ferment, many of the Scandinavians still considered themselves to be rustic — for instance, the Danish writer Georg Brandes (1842-1927) reflected, "In the North, one had the feeling of being shut off from the intellectual life of the time." Indeed, many of the region's great artists decided to spend the greater part of their careers abroad, searching for a livelihood.

But the latter part of the 19th century saw a much larger exodus of people: the massive emigration to the United States and Canada, popularly — if somewhat melodramatically — known

In a tempera painting by the Finnish artist Gallén-Kallela, the jealous Joukahainen waits, bow in hand, to ambush Väinämöinen, the hero of Finland's national epic, the *Kalevala*. This compilation of ballads, published in 1835, inspired a new awareness of Finnish language and culture.

2

as the "Great Bloodletting." As the populations of Sweden, Denmark, Norway and Finland virtually doubled between 1800 and 1900, so did the pressure on available resources. For peasants from the rocky and unyielding soils of Småland in southern Sweden and Danes from the barren heathland of Jutland, leaving their homelands seemed to be the only solution.

In 1870, one in 10 of all immigrants to the United States came from the Scandinavian countries, and the flood did not subside until the beginning of World War I. Among them were many Finnish and Norwegian farmers, who were driven from their homes by the periodic famines that still ravaged northern agriculture.

In the lands they had left behind, the seeds of social change were being planted. Thanks to agricultural improvements, such as the increasing consumption of potatoes and other new root crops, people were better nourished than ever before. They were also healthier: The Jenner method of vaccination against smallpox, introduced to Scandinavia at the beginning of the 19th century, was gradually liberating northerners from the ravages of their most dreaded disease. The effect of smallpox on small, ill-fed communities had always been devastating; in an 18th-century epidemic, for instance, Iceland lost an estimated one third of its total population.

With the coming of railroads to Denmark in the 1840s and the development of fast, efficient steamships that could ply the fjords of Norway, forge more reliable links with Iceland, and wend their way between the islands off the Danish and Swedish coasts, communications improved beyond measure. New technologies and products were

Haakon VII, first king of an independent Norway for 500 years, poses with Queen Maud and Prince Olav for a portrait in 1909. A Danish prince, Haakon was offered the throne by the Norwegian parliament after the union with Sweden ended in 1905.

carried to the rural hinterlands by the same ships and trains that took people away from the countryside to the more promising economic prospects of the new industrial towns.

New ideas, and ideals, were in the air: the right for a people to direct affairs of state through democratically elected representatives, the fairer distribution of the burden of taxation, the reform of old laws restricting ownership of property. By the 1880s, both Denmark and Sweden had witnessed the birth of modern political parties — Social Democrats, Liberals, Conservatives. In Finland, the 1906 constitution put that small, relatively backward state into the political vanguard by granting women the right to vote — the first European nation to do so.

Meanwhile, in Norway, the most pressing issue of the day was the struggle for national independence, after half a millennium of rule by its neighboring countries. The increasingly restive, separatist Norwegians had never quite reconciled themselves to living

under the Swedish crown, and a series of relatively minor issues eventually led to a formal rupture.

The Norwegian merchant marine, for example, had become one of the world's largest: Were its ships entitled to fly a Norwegian rather than a Swedish flag? And was the theoretically separate and equal kingdom of Norway entitled to establish its own consular offices wherever it chose to do so? The Swedish reply to such questions was invariably in the negative.

By 1905, Norwegian irritation had reached such a pitch that the nation's parliamentary body — the Storting — ordained a plebiscite on the question of whether to dissolve the union with Sweden. The vote was 368,211 in favor of dissolution and only 184 against it. Sweden did not demur.

After the king of Sweden had formally relinquished his Norwegian crown, the Storting elected a member of the Danish royal family, Prince Carl, to the throne of Norway. In choosing to reign as Haakon VII, he reached across more than 500 years of history to adopt the name of the last of the native Norse kings, Haakon VI, who had ruled Norway at the end of the 14th century.

During World War I, Norway, Denmark and Sweden remained determinedly neutral, and they were thus spared the bloodshed that decimated the major belligerents. But Iceland, after having been separated from Denmark by four years of British and German blockade, had grown accustomed to running its own affairs: After the war, it insisted on becoming a sovereign state, maintaining its ties to Denmark only by a common monarchy.

Meanwhile, events on the eastern front were pushing Finland toward independence. The Revolution of 1917 threw Russia into chaos, and the Finns took this opportunity to make their own bid for sovereignty.

On December 6, 1917, Finland became an independent republic. But it then suffered a bloody civil war because the Bolshevik Red brigades wanted to set up a Communist government in Finland. They were defeated by the Nationalist Whites led by General Carl Gustaf Mannerheim, a Swedo-Finnish nobleman who had served with distinction in the tsarist army.

In 1920, the Soviet government formalized relations with the newly independent Finland, recognizing a Russo-Finnish border, a part of which, in Soviet eyes, ran menacingly close to Leningrad. But less than 20 years elapsed before Europe again became a powder keg, giving Russia an opportunity to revise the boundary.

After Hitler and Stalin had divided conquered Poland in 1939, at the outset of World War II, the U.S.S.R. invaded Finland with 26 to 29 divisions. To everyone's astonishment, the Soviets were repulsed by a far smaller Finnish force, consisting of only nine divisions, again led by General Mannerheim. Still, after successfully defending most of her territory in the 1939-1940 Winter War, Finland was ultimately unable to maintain its resistance against the superior strength of its giant neighbor and was forced to grant the Soviet Union major territorial concessions along the Eastern frontiers.

Almost simultaneously, Scandinavian neutrality was breached a second time when Hitler's armies invaded both Denmark and Norway. In response, the British (who were subsequently replaced by the Americans) occupied Iceland. The Danish government capitulated almost at once to German threats of bombing Copenhagen. The Norwegians fought a bold delaying action that was doomed to failure, because the fall of France forced the British to withdraw the expeditionary force they had sent to support them. Danes and Norwegians had to live under the control of German occupation regimes for the remainder of the war.

Sweden maintained a tenuous and rather one-sided neutrality. The nation kept this precarious status by allowing German troops on leave to move through its territory and by supplying critical material for the German war machine from mines and factories.

When Hitler invaded the U.S.S.R., Finland became a "cobelligerent" in an effort to win back lost territories; but after the German armies began to collapse in 1944, Finland had to change sides and become a cobelligerent of the Allies, fighting to expel the German troops who were making a last stand in the north of the peninsula.

In Norway, the Nazis installed a puppet government under the fascist politician Quisling — a name that was to enter the dictionary as a synonym for turncoat and traitor. His murderous police state was actively resisted by one of the toughest and most effective underground movements in Europe, directed from London by a Norwegian government-in-exile headed by the aging but determined Haakon VII.

The king of Denmark had remained in Copenhagen, where his steadfast conduct during the war set his subjects an example of personal and passive resistance to the German occupation. For a time, Denmark as a whole seemed sufficiently obedient to qualify as Hitler's "model protectorate." But as the war progressed, the Danish resistance movement, like the Norwegian, began to play an active part in sabotaging rail lines and communications in preparation for the Allied liberation of Europe. Among other achievements, it succeeded in saving virtually all of Denmark's Jews from Hitler's "final solution" by smuggling them to safety in neutral Sweden before they could be rounded up by the Germans.

During the summer of 1944, distant Iceland severed its links with Denmark by dissolving the common monarchy and declaring itself an independent republic. When peace came in 1945, Finland found itself still further reduced in size and forced to pay massive reparations to the Soviet Union for its part in the war. Norway, too, had suffered heavy casualties and had lost half its merchant fleet, which was used to carry vital Allied cargoes across the Atlantic Ocean. Its two northernmost counties were destroyed by the Germans' scorched-earth policy, which wiped out roads, flattened buildings and returned the land to a state of near-medieval poverty and desolation.

Altogether, Scandinavia had borne more than its share of the sufferings inflicted by Hitler's war. Yet no part of Europe was quicker to recover its social and economic energies. Indeed, postwar Scandinavia was to become in many respects a model for the rest of Europe — with its democratic politics, its social conscience, and its leadership in architecture and design, art and international affairs.

Again, as so often in the past, the Scandinavians were able to exercise an influence on the rest of the world that was far out of proportion to their numbers. The once-unknown North was no longer the Ultima Thule of civilization, but one of the most vital and creative regions in the family of nations. □

SCANDINAVIA UNDER SIEGE

At the outbreak of World War II in September 1939, the small nations of Scandinavia immediately declared their neutrality and prayed for the storm to pass them by. The well-armed Swedes were, indeed, to be spared. But for their weaker neighbors — the Finns, the Danes and the Norwegians — the days ahead were anguishing.

The first victims were the Finns, who woke on November 30 to find themselves under attack by the Red Army. Although the Russians were still neutral at this time, they wanted to take over part of the Finnish border as a buffer against a possible attack by Germany. Undeterred by the massive odds against them, the Finns fought back with terrifying ferocity, inflicting 10 Soviet casualties for every one of their own.

The Finns, however, were unable to make up their losses, and in March 1940, they were forced to accept the Soviet territorial demands. But peace was to be short-lived, because in June 1941, when Hitler finally attacked the Soviet Union, the Finns joined the Germans. In the subsequent fray, nearly three million troops saw action on Finnish soil — more than in any other Scandinavian nation.

Meanwhile, Denmark and Norway were undergoing their own ordeals. In the spring of 1940, with little warning, Hitler's forces swiftly occupied the two countries. At first, people were too stunned to react. But, as the shock of defeat wore off, defiance of the invaders increased. Unable to match the German war machine on its own terms, many civilians became part-time guerrillas, ambushing German soldiers, destroying military installations, and blowing up roads and railroads. In the first four months of 1945 alone, the Danes carried out some 2,000 separate sabotage operations.

The price of freedom was high, and thousands of Danish and Norwegian patriots were either shot or deported. But repression merely intensified the flame of resistance — a flame that burned throughout the five dark years of the Occupation.

With their equipment loaded on reindeer-hauled sledges, Finnish ski troops move through Lapland during the Winter War against the U.S.S.R. in 1939-1940. So silent was their approach and so expert their marksmanship that some Russians nicknamed them Belaya Smert — the White Death.

A German parachutist floats down to earth near Narvik in northern Norway during the German assault of 1940. Hitler's war machine demanded supplies of Swedish iron ore; Narvik was the principal port through which it flowed to Germany.

Reduced to rubble after 30 minutes of bombing, a Norwegian town is overrun by German infantry. With more than 400 warplanes at their disposal, the Germans took town after town in the same way, occupying most of southern Norway in 25 days.

Battle-weary soldiers of the Wehrmacht rest outside a bakery in Norway. Despite the intervention of Allied forces, the Germans completed their conquest in a lightning two-month campaign, described by Hitler as "one of the sauciest undertakings in the history of modern warfare."

Mingling with the crowds, two German soldiers inspect the day's catch at the fish market in occupied Copenhagen. At first, the Danes responded to their invaders with icy politeness, but by 1943, the underground had become so disruptive that the Germans declared martial law throughout the country.

Evicted from their Oslo apartment to make room for billeted German troops, a Norwegian mother and child wait as their possessions are loaded on moving vans. Such citizens not only had to find new accommodations, but they also had to go on paying the rent for the old.

A dentist's office serves as a makeshift composing room for the journal *Free Denmark* — one of more than 300 Danish underground papers that appeared during the German occupation. In the event of a Gestapo raid, the trays of type and printing plates could be swiftly slipped into secret cupboards.

A boy flees as Danish saboteurs blow up a German-run munitions factory in Copenhagen in the summer of 1944. With the workers safely evacuated, a 30-man assault team set off five explosions that destroyed the plant.

A Nazi flag is burned in Copenhagen during a nationwide strike called to coincide with the Allied invasion of Normandy in June 1944. Although the week-long strike helped to delay German troop movements from Denmark to France, it also led to serious fighting in which 100 Danes were killed.

Flag-waving women in rapturous celebration parade down a Copenhagen street on May 5, 1945, following the surrender of the German forces in Denmark. Two days later, the German army in Norway capitulated.

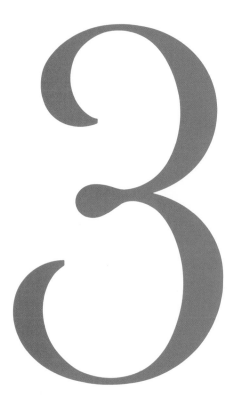

A LIFE GEARED TO TWO SEASONS

In one of Scandinavia's favorite fairy tales — Sampo Lappelil, or "Sampo, the Little Lapp Boy" — the King of the Trolls proclaims at midwinter that he has killed the sun and that henceforth he will rule over a world of darkness and cold. His troll subjects, who are gathered by the thousands around the icy peak that serves as his throne, immediately send up a great cry of approval because, like all trolls, they regard the sun as being synonymous with death. According to legend, these malevolent creatures are doomed to explode into smithereens or turn into stone if they should ever be exposed to the light of the sun.

The fable could not be more artfully designed to impress on Scandinavian children the totally alien nature of the trolls, because the trolls' reaction to the king's declaration is exactly opposite that of humankind. Throughout the Nordic countries, virtually all children grow up in an environment where everyone truly mourns the autumnal decline of the sun. For Scandinavians, sunshine is synonymous with life — something to be cherished, pursued and exploited. During the winter, they seek their sun-god (Baldur, as he was known to their pagan ancestors) on the shores of the Mediterranean, the Canaries and the Azores, where there are many apartments and hotels that are owned or operated by Nordic companies. And in the summer, as soon as the sun gathers strength, they take ev-ery conceivable opportunity to get out of doors and luxuriate in its warmth.

It is not so much the heat of the sun that matters to Scandinavians; more important to them is the duration of light that summer bestows, the longed-for release from winter's darkness. Each year, the lengthening nights of winter are anticipated on All Saints' Day, November 1, a public holiday recognized by northern inhabitants as the beginning of what Norwegians call *mørketiden*, or "the murky time," and the Finns call *kaamosaika*, or "the dark time." In the extreme north, a period of darkness relieved only briefly by twilight has already begun. The Polar Eskimos of northwest Greenland, members of the northernmost community on earth, experience four months without sunlight, from late October to February. In mainland Scandinavia, in such northerly places as Tromso and Hammerfest in Norway and Utsjoki and Ivalo in Finland, the sun is below the horizon for six weeks or more, from the beginning of December. And in Iceland and Norway, generally, the gloom is deepened by frequent cloud cover. Even in southerly Scandinavian cities such as Oslo, Stockholm and Helsinki, it is at least 9 a.m. before street lights are extinguished in midwinter, and they come on again at 3 p.m.

Darkness has always been a symbol of these high-latitude lands. The Nordic territories were known as the "midnight lands" by the inhabitants of medi-

Glowing above the trampled winter snow, posters advertising Mediterranean vacations line a bus shelter in Helsinki. A winter package-tour to sunny climates is considered essential by many Scandinavians, who spend much more money on trips abroad than they earn from tourism at home.

3

eval Europe—long before the tourist industry glowingly popularized them as the "lands of the midnight sun." To 17th-century Germans, Gustavus Adolphus was *Der Löwe von Mitternach* —the Lion of Midnight, rather than the Lion of the North. And in Finland, a two- or three-day-old child used to be called a two- or three-night child if born in midwinter.

Darkness has long haunted the artists of Scandinavia, too. Cold and gloom are blamed for deaths in plays by Ibsen. They are symbols in *The House in the Dark,* a saga about the German occupation of Norway by leading Norwegian novelist Tarje Vesaas. They are part of the powerful chiaroscuro of the Finnish poet Eino Leino, and they are inherent in the work of Swedish director Ingmar Bergman—sometimes in the very titles of his films: *Through a Glass Darkly* and *Winter Light.*

Beyond Denmark, where the climate is more closely related to that of the Netherlands and northeast Germany, the fleeting Nordic seasons of spring and autumn merge so closely with winter that it is possible to speak of a three-part winter: autumn-winter (October and November), high winter (December through February) and spring-winter (March and April). Of the three, autumn-winter generally seems the most depressing time, since it offers only the promise of another prolonged period of cold and darkness ahead.

A few years ago during *kaamosaika*, a Finnish psychiatrist, Erkki Väisänen of the University of Oulu, studied Finns in a small northern town and found signs of more depression and higher incidence of alcohol abuse and suicide than in the summer. Similar evidence of lower spirits was found by American journalist Edwin Kiester Jr. when he ob-

served life in the Norwegian city of Tromso during *mørketiden.* He also found, to his surprise, that the most common complaint was insomnia. "Over and over I heard the same lament. People slept fine in the summer, but, as darkness began, they couldn't fall asleep at night. When they would finally doze off, they couldn't rouse themselves in the morning." Pharmacists confirmed that prescriptions for sleeping pills increased by one third during "the murky time." And studies indicated that about one fourth of Tromso's population of 46,000 had complaints of sleeplessness at this season, the problem being most prevalent among young adults.

The reaction to autumn-winter is much less pronounced farther south. Nevertheless, throughout Scandinavia, it remains the most unpopular time of year. High winter, to be sure, brings the longest nights, but this can be darkness of a less gloomy kind. The coming of snow contributes a certain luminosity to the land; nights can have a magical quality when the full light of the moon and the stars are reflected and intensified by snow and ice. High winter is also the time when the aurora borealis, the northern lights, can be seen most vividly. This phenomenon, caused by light emitted from the upper atmosphere as showers of subatomic particles from the sun pass through, takes the shape of banners or arches of light in the night sky—reddish and bluish as well as white—and is most often visible in northern Norway.

Spring-winter, too, has its drawbacks. Frozen waters become treacherous, and city snow turns to brown slush. In many parts, a Scandinavian spring day will fit the description given by Norway's celebrated author Olav Dunn

in his novel *The Floodtide of Fate:* "mud all over the roads and yellow-gray slush all over the fields." But whatever the conditions, at least there is always the supreme consolation that summer cannot be far behind.

There are marked variations in the severity of winter in different parts of Scandinavia. For example, temperatures of -30° F. are not unknown in Finnish Lapland and Swedish Norrbotten. Meanwhile, owing to the moderating effect of the Gulf Stream, it may be only a few degrees below freezing in Reykjavik and slightly above freezing in Bergen. Nevertheless, the fact remains that at least half of the surface area of Scandinavia is covered by snow for six months or longer in most years. Average snow depths can vary greatly — from well over three feet in much of Norway, which is exposed to wet, westerly winds, to less than eight inches in parts of Finland that are sheltered by the Scandinavian mountains.

The intensity of sea ice is similarly variable. Along the Atlantic coastline of the Scandinavian countries, it is slight; and here the saline waters of the outer ocean remain free of ice. On the other hand, every winter—for a minimum of a month or two in the southwest and for about four or five months in the north—ice forms along the thousands of miles of Finland's intricate coastline. And the situation is the same along Sweden's Bothnian coast.

On land, frost may penetrate deeply into the soil—up to three feet in the peat lands of much of Scandinavia. And sometimes, high-pressure systems build up over the continental land mass and create so-called iron winters. Then the entire Baltic Sea and the waters that separate Denmark and Sweden may freeze over; landscape and seascape

On Norway's Lofoten Islands, a young boy leans on a *sparkstotting*, one of three standing idle in the snow. The *spark* resembles a wooden chair on runners, and it is widely used in northern Scandinavia for carrying children and packages through the snow.

will resemble those of the Ice Age, and ice floes may still be drifting in the Gulf of Bothnia at midsummer.

The contrast between summer and winter is, for most Scandinavians, highly dramatic. "Winter is a certainty," wrote the Finnish author Toivo Pekkanen; "summer is an illusion." Other than flying south, there is no escaping winter, whereas summer — illusion or not — is a season to be welcomed with almost reckless abandon. In response to these climatic extremes, two ways of life have emerged. One is geared toward combating the winter and, wherever possible, capitalizing on its few advantageous characteristics. The other is bent on exploiting the brief summer to the maximum.

"Winter is the element for which we are born," wrote the 19th-century Finnish historian Zachris Topelius. And certainly it is still the element that has the most profound influence on the lifestyle of Scandinavians. That style, however, has changed almost beyond recognition since the time of Topelius, when agriculture was the primary activity and most of the family stayed indoors as much as possible during winter to conserve energy and food. Today, modern technology enables the Scandinavians to achieve victory on many fronts in their relentless war on winter's darkness and cold.

Since the coming of electricity in the late 19th century, they have increasingly challenged the darkness with an extravagance of light. Floodlighting is widely used for public buildings; neon lighting is more than generously employed for advertisements; and arc lamps seem to be twice as numerous as in other lands. Indeed, to fly over Norway, Sweden or Finland on a clear winter's night is to be aware of a surprisingly extensive pattern of lights for such thinly populated territory. Almost all Scandinavian homes — even the remotest farmsteads of Iceland — are now supplied with electricity, and many householders use it with little thought of economizing.

Scandinavians are no less extravagant with heating. The majority live in a centrally heated environment and use some degree of heating for nine months of the year. As costs of fuels steadily rise, however, every possible form of heat conservation is practiced. Double glazing has been commonly replaced by triple glazing. In some homes, metal-plated window glass serves to reflect interior heat. Thick insulating layers of fiberglass and other materials fill city walls and roofs; and where there are fireplaces and stoves, dampers prevent the entry of cold air. Usually double doors are provided, even in private homes, and in many public buildings the main doors are so heavy that it is a struggle to open them.

Nevertheless, domestic heating and lighting are still a huge expense, and inevitably the need is greatest in the least privileged areas — the thinly populated expanses of northern Sweden, Norway and Finland and the remoter coastal settlements of Iceland. In Finland, however, there is a government heating allowance for people in high latitudes, and it is geared to the average number of days in a year — anywhere from 150 to 200 — when the temperature falls below freezing.

Clothing is another punishment on the purse in winter. The contrast between the airless 70° F. of centrally heated indoors and the subzero outdoors calls for heavy overcoats, furs (with the added cost of insurance and summer storage), knee-high boots and that most dreary of footwear — galoshes. Fur hats are *de rigueur* — earflapped for military conscripts, wolfskin for dashing youths, mink for matrons and sealskin for men. Again, those who live and work in the most inclement areas incur the greatest expense and the cost is so heavy that civil servants in the regions farthest north get a winter clothing allowance.

For young and old alike, waterproof

Brightly lit windows accentuate the cold and dark that shroud Tromso on an afternoon in early January *(left)*. On the 21st of the month — Sol Dag, or Sun Day — children in a warm classroom *(below)* celebrate the return of daylight with a display of paper suns.

WAGING WAR ON WINTER GLOOM

In the Norwegian town of Tromso, almost 200 miles above the Arctic Circle, the sun sets on November 25 and does not reappear for nearly two months. During this dark time, the town's 46,000 inhabitants fight depression by keeping their houses brightly lighted and leading a gregarious life: An average Tromso family uses 20 percent more electricity than one in the south of the country, and there are more restaurant seats per capita than in any other Norwegian town.

The ordeal ends at last on the 21st of January when the sun briefly rises again, bringing four minutes of daylight and a welcome release from gloom.

3

and windproof artificial fabrics have greatly helped the winter wardrobe. Nevertheless, winter wear does impose a variety of problems and demands. Since winter is very much the season for entertaining at home in Scandinavia, even the most modest apartment has a closet near the entrance to receive the clutter of coats, overshoes and shoe bags. Theaters and concert halls have armies of well-trained coatroom attendants; restaurants usually have a fixed charge for accommodating winter clothing in their coatrooms. Shopping in an overheated supermarket while wearing outdoor clothing can be a very sweaty business.

Various other costs and chores are necessitated by the winter cold. Householders with gardens need to protect their roses, shrubs and other less hardy plants in wrappings of straw, burlap or paper. Except in the more favored areas, such as Denmark and the western coastlands of Norway and Sweden, lawns require reseeding after the spring thaw. At the water's edge, millions of pleasure boats must be provided with winter accommodation. The majority of motorists need to fit their cars with snow tires to reduce the risk of skidding on icy roads, and in most modern residences the car is treated to a centrally heated garage.

At the national level, the cost of fighting winter can be astronomical. It is estimated that the war on winter consumes at least 5 percent of Finland's gross domestic product. No one can afford to gamble on a mild winter; all investment is in anticipation of severe conditions. Road, railroad and airport maintenance calls for snow plows, snow blowers, special heaters, snow fences and (in Norway) hundreds of miles of snow sheds to protect mountain rail-

road tracks from drifts and avalanches. Norway has by far the greatest problem with snow accumulation. As recently as a generation ago, it was rare for continuous road communication to be maintained between eastern and western Norway in the winter. Today, only one major route is likely to be kept open during a hard winter — the main highway across the Hardangervidda, which links Oslo with Bergen.

Of the Scandinavian countries, excluding Denmark, Finland is the least affected by snow. Nevertheless, its central road authority musters some 1,600 snow plows and maintains more than 2,100 miles of snow fences to prevent drifting across road surfaces. In towns, snow removal keeps an army of laborers busy. In Helsinki, emergency clearance may be undertaken by local landowners, who use their own tractors and trailers to cart snow to one of the city's mountainous snow dumps. Caretakers, tethered to chimney stacks and other structures for safety, clamber over

rooftops to clear them of snow before avalanches descend on passing pedestrians. But it is impossible to keep roads and sidewalks free of ice, and every year in Helsinki alone hundreds of people suffer broken bones.

Such weather conditions impose great restraints on any outdoor activity and make for seasonal unemployment and underemployment. (The construction industry is especially vulnerable.) The labor problem is addressed by unemployment compensation; by insurance payments; and by subsidies for construction activity, which help offset the extra costs of keeping the work going during winter. In some cases, continuity can be maintained by providing a heated environment. In towns of central Finland and north Sweden, office, apartment and public buildings under construction may be wrapped in plastic, while hot-air blowers boost the inside temperature to allow work with concrete, cement and bricklaying. Some work sites are covered permanently, among them one of Wärtsila's shipyards in Helsinki, which embraces a dock capable of accommodating vessels of more than 20,000 tons.

There can be no such protection for forest workers. The felling of conifers is always confined to periods when snow is on the ground, to facilitate hauling. Inevitably, at such times, low temperatures and blizzards frequently interrupt schedules. But at least working conditions have been greatly eased by mechanization — the power saws, tractors, and mechanical equipment for loading and bundling. In prewar years, after the first heavy falls of snow, tens of thousands of lumberjacks migrated with their horses to the woodlands of northern Sweden and Finland. Then, for four or five months, they existed under fairly primitive conditions, living in huge communal huts and trekking increasingly great distances to work as they cleared the nearest forest. Today, as a result of mechanized harvesting, far fewer workers are needed, and mobile homes are used to reduce the number of journeys to and from the working area. Moreover, such amenities as the base camps are now rigorously controlled by state legislation: Buildings must conform to precise standards; there is a staff that provides meals; sanitation is strictly monitored; and to reduce the risk of brawls, alcohol is banned.

Winter presents an even greater challenge for those who earn their living at sea. Until the coming of steel-plated steamships in the late 19th century, most Scandinavian vessels were laid up for six months, and Iceland suffered a break in communications for several consecutive months every year. Storms and gales regularly caused disasters. Not surprisingly, the legend of the Flying Dutchman had its setting around the skerries of western Norway. And one of Europe's most notorious graveyards of shipping is sited off the Danish Skaw, where the masts and bulkheads of wrecked vessels still testify to hundreds of tragedies. Indeed, one of the reasons for the construction in the 1890s of the Kiel Canal, cutting across the neck of the Jutland peninsula in northern Germany, was to provide a sheltered route for shipping to pass from the North Sea to the Baltic Sea.

It is little more than a century since Sweden made the first tentative efforts to maintain continuous winter communication with Finland and the island of Gotland by way of steamboats. In the early 1890s, the first crude antecedents of the modern icebreakers were introduced. Now Finland has a fleet of about 10 major icebreakers, supplemented by a number of smaller vessels, which clear ice in and around the most important harbors. Sweden has seven icebreakers and Denmark four; however, since 1961, there has been a formal agreement for cooperation in the employment of icebreaker fleets among Norway, Denmark, Sweden and Finland. The Finnish icebreaker fleet also cooperates with icebreakers from the Soviet Union in the Gulf of Finland.

The strategy of Finland and Sweden is to concentrate icebreaker operations initially in the Gulf of Bothnia. But here the battle is often lost. The northern Bothnian ports, such as Lulea, Kemi and Oulu, are liable to be closed for four months, starting in early January. When this happens, the icebreaker fleet moves south and devotes most of its efforts to keeping open the channels for the shipping that uses the leading export harbors of Kotka, Hamina, Rauma, Turku and Helsinki. On the Swedish side of the gulf, ports south of Umea are not normally affected by icing to a serious degree. As the thaw sets in, the fleet can transfer its attention to hastening the reopening of the northern Bothnian ports.

In severe winters, it is still possible for ferries to be trapped in the ice of the central Baltic, and even icebreakers may have great difficulty keeping on the move. The most critical time of year is late February to late March; then, icebreaker crews — each with about 40 men, plus a few women who are employed in the catering service — may work for two or three weeks without a break. Technically, icebreakers could maintain continuity of shipping to all Finnish and Swedish harbors. However, this is not attempted because it is cheaper either to export to the nearest open harbor or to stockpile goods before the big freeze sets in.

The development of ice forecasting has been another key aid to Scandinavian shipping in winter. Finland and Sweden have been accumulating information on the behavior of ice in the Baltic basin for well over half a century; in the 1930s, Finland prepared the first ice atlas of the Baltic, with a vocabulary of ice types and forms. Now it is possible to make predictions of ice formation and movement based on clearly identifiable weather patterns. Wind direction is particularly important once ice has begun to form: The prevailing Westerly winds, for example, cause ice floes to drift away from the Swedish coast and to form pack ice along the Finnish shores.

Weekly ice charts are produced for all of the Baltic area, and daily situation reports are provided for the approaches to the principal harbors. Formerly, they were compiled from the reports of icebreakers, merchant and naval ships, aircraft and lighthouses. Today, satellite photography is a principal source of information.

While Finnish and Swedish ports on the Gulf of Bothnia may be closed by ice for months, Norwegian ships are able to operate throughout winter on the western side of mainland Scandinavia. Indeed, for at least a millennium, between February and April each year, fishermen have reaped an extraordinary cod harvest in ice-free Vest Fjord, on the northwest coast of Norway. Vest Fjord is protected on its north and west sides by the 93-mile-long wall of the Lofoten Islands, whose jagged peaks soar upward like the spines of a gigantic dragon's back; and here, warmer waters of the Gulf Stream mingle with the

3

cooler waters of Arctic Norway to produce outstanding conditions for the production of plankton, the tiny creatures that are the main food of the cod.

A thousand years ago, on a visit to Alfred, King of Wessex in England, the north Norwegian trader Othere made the first recorded report of the fishing bonanza at this supreme cod feeding ground. Today, the spectacle is still astonishing: Vessels of all shapes, sizes and colors bob on the water for as far as the eye can see, all set against a dramatic backcloth of snow-clad pinnacles. Ashore, fish are beheaded and gutted and hung on fish racks to dry, or filleted and frozen for the international market. Fish-meal and cod-liver-oil factories belch out their unsavory odors, and down in the harbors a vast company of followers afloat await the return of the fishing fleet: hospital ships, generator ships, Salvation Army ships, tourist and entertainment ships, some of which even carry all the paraphernalia of a traveling circus. With some justification, the annual Lofoten harvest has been called "the greatest fishing show on earth."

Winter gives a certain grim earnestness to daily life in the greater part of Scandinavia, but it also yields distinct forms of relaxation and enjoyment. Winter is the season when social life reaches a climax. As soon as people have cast off the melancholy of autumn, they plunge into a round of parties, visits to friends, and outings to the plays and concerts that are staged in even the smallest towns. For Norwegians, Swedes and Finns, winter sports facilities are available on virtually every doorstep. And winter is a time of numerous festivals and anniversary days.

On Father's Day (the second Sunday in November), candles appear on graves all over Finland, and they illuminate all war cemeteries on Independence Day (December 6). In Sweden, the festival season starts on December 13, St. Lucia's Day, when throughout the land, white-robed Lucias wear crowns with circlets of lighted candles. Then, accompanied by candle-bearing attendants and boys carrying starred wands, they sing in a procession on their way with coffee and cakes to the elders of countless households. Candles are invariably lighted, too, when guests are entertained for a meal. And, of course, in anticipation of Yuletide (*Jul* is the old Scandinavian word for the Christmas season), candlelit or electric-lit fir trees spring up in every street and home. Most Danish homes also display a wreath of pine twigs decorated with four candles, and over all of Scandinavia, at social gatherings, homes are further illuminated when akvavit is set aflame on top of the mulled wine, yielding a beverage with the warming name of *glögg*.

It seems natural that these lands of Christmas trees and reindeer should have become the presumed home of Father Christmas. Yet Santa Claus is essentially an import as far as Scandinavians are concerned. Their own native Christmastide visitor is the nisse, or brownie — a good-humored household sprite with short legs, a long flowing beard and a red-tasseled cap who is reckoned to be several thousand years old. Fifty years ago it was rare to see a nisse, although one might be lured to the doorstep by a bowl of porridge put out on Christmas Eve. Today in Iceland, the first nisses are said to arrive 13 days before Christmas and remain until the first week of the New Year. Elsewhere in Scandinavia, nisses seem to have lost their shyness and to have yielded to the temptations of the commercial world. They appear on the streets carrying advertising signs, and they haunt the department stores, especially in the toy sections.

Despite his foreign origins, Santa Claus is now an established Scandinavian institution, and there are children worldwide who locate his home in the capital of Finnish Lapland, Rovaniemi, a city of 30,000 people in which the postal authorities have generously accepted the responsibility of answering mail addressed to him. Some other children locate his home in Greenland or Iceland instead. And, not to be outdone, an American entrepreneur has sensed a potential for profit in Santaland, a Disney-style tourist complex comprising the home and workshops of Father Christmas, as well as such garish attractions as the Palace of the Snow Queen and Dinosaur Park. Despite a good deal of opposition, Santaland has been created in Gesunda, a village of 300 people overlooking Siljan, one of Sweden's most beautiful lakes, in the resort area of Dalarna.

By the time of the Christmas holiday, the most welcome bonus of the long winter is being enjoyed: the three- or four-month skiing season. In Norway, Sweden and Finland, most citizens can enjoy virtually unimpeded cross-country skiing from their street corner, if not from their doorstep. In the words of a suburban Stockholmer, "There is nothing to stop you from skiing from here to Lapland." Children are put on skis as soon as they can walk and, as the late President Kekkonen of Finland demonstrated, some devotees continue skiing into their eighties or later. In Finland alone, more than one million skiers — fully a quarter of the total pop-

Standing on a beam, a fishery worker hangs cod on a rack to dry — a simple method of preserving. Because of the increased use of refrigeration, traditional drying racks are declining in number but are still used in the Lofoten Islands *(below)*, one of the richest breeding grounds for cod.

ulation — are in possession of proficiency certificates issued by the national skiing society, recognizing that they have mastered the basics of the sport. There are skiing competitions in innumerable Finnish, Norwegian and Swedish towns, and ski jumps are provided by the thousands.

This winter bonus originated long ago. Ski-type wooden runners, dated by carbon analysis as being six to seven thousand years old, have been recovered from bogs in Sweden and Finland, as well as from the surface of a Norwegian glacier. But it is impossible to tell how effectively they were used. Certainly, high-speed competitive skiing — as we know it today — did not begin until the mid-19th century, when Sondre Norheim, a farmer from the district of Telemark, introduced a stiff binding around the heel, fastening the foot to the ski in much the same way as a skate is fastened, and so making it possible to turn and jump. Previously, for thousands of years, skiers had used only a toe strap, which gave only a little maneuverability.

As a result of heel-binding, the slalom and jumping developed rapidly. In the 1880s, skiing competitions began almost simultaneously in Sweden, Finland and Norway; and from the beginning, there were women participants. A. E. Nordenskjöld, the scientist and arctic explorer who led the first expedition through the Northeast Passage, is usually credited with the foundation of official skiing contests in Sweden in 1884. One of his ardent admirers, Fridtjof Nansen, the first man to cross Greenland on skis, did much to popularize the sport in his native Norway.

Today, the ski season has a number of climaxes. In the Swedish region of Dalarna, on the first Sunday in

March, thousands participate in the 90-kilometer (56-mile) Vasa race, which commemorates the occasion in 1521 when men from Dalarna skied to Norway to ask Gustavus Vasa, the future king of Sweden, to return as their leader. In Norway, the competitions staged at Holmenkollen's sky-high ski jump gain worldwide television coverage, and every year large crowds gather to watch the major events of the Finnish winter sporting calendar at Lahti. Schools usually enjoy ski vacations in February; and when Easter falls early in the year, almost all active Norwegians take to the slopes for the last great vacation of the winter. As spring approaches, enthusiasts follow the skiing northward, to the fells of Lapland. And

even in summer the action continues. Dedicated skiers travel to the snowfields of western Norway's largest glacier, 315-square-mile Jostedalsbre, for competitions in July. Others, to keep their muscles in shape, embark upon wheeled skis, thrusting themselves along footpaths and country roads.

Ice provides a setting for other winter activities, but it no longer rivals snow. Now that most people can afford high-class ski equipment, ice-skating does not attract quite such a following as it had in the 1930s, in the heyday of Norway's Sonja Henie. At that time, it was the great Scandinavian dream to emulate the success of the incomparable Oslo girl who became world figure-skating champion at the age of 13, re-

One of Finland's thousands of dedicated skiers keeps in summer trim with the aid of wheeled skis on a forest road. More than 100 annual cross-country treks and marathons, each attracting up to 4,000 entrants, encourage a competitive attitude toward skiing.

tained the title for 10 successive years, won three Olympic championships, then emigrated to Hollywood to become a multimillion-dollar movie star.

Ice hockey, however, is increasingly popular in Norway, Sweden and Finland, and winter trotting races on ice-covered lakes have become a regular country sport. Iceboating, which originated in the early 17th century, still has a following. And, for the more sedentary, ice fishing is as popular as ever. Only the approach to this activity has changed. In days past, those who went ice fishing were hoping to catch something to eat. Their modern counterparts — with their tents, protective clothing, heaters and a little warming alcohol — are simply enjoying a hobby. In Finland, a national ice-fishing competition attracts as many as 5,000 competitors every year.

Autumn-winter is the main hunting season in the north, where elk have become the principal quarry. Their sheer numbers, together with the damage they cause to growing timber and the danger they present to motorists, have made them something of a menace in Sweden and Finland. Consequently, every year more than 70,000 licenses to kill them are issued in Finland, and many more in Sweden.

In Lapland, wolf packs — some of them intruding from the vast forests of the Soviet Union — can be a threat to the domesticated reindeer. They are pursued by helicopter as well as by hunters on skis. Winter seal hunting, once a significant seasonal activity in the Bothnian islands, also continues, but not only in the Vaasa archipelago. It is estimated that there are some 20,000 seals in these waters, and they

are the principal predators upon the valuable salmon. They are pursued in traditional style by white-camouflaged hunters who move on skis, dragging sleighs on which to carry their quarry back to the mainland.

Scandinavia's hunting season comes to an end with the arrival of spring-winter and the long, gradual thaw. In late April, in the woodlands of Sweden and Finland, the sky-blue *Anemone hepatica* and the first mouse-eared birch leaves are the harbingers of the new season. Among the oak and beech woods of Denmark, the bluebells are in bloom. In general, however, the Scandinavian spring is noted more for disruption than for visual attractions. In Norway, Sweden and Finland, the awesome thunder of *islossning* — the break-up of river ice — warns the people of imminent floods. In the mountains of

CELEBRATIONS OF MIDSUMMER

On Lake Siljan, in the Swedish region of Dalarna, a traditional "church boat" carries women in local dress to a Midsummer service. Two fiddlers sit in the boat's bow, while the minister waves from the stern.

In lands of winter darkness, there is special reason to celebrate the longest day of summer. Throughout Scandinavia, Midsummer Eve is marked — as it has been for centuries — by music, merry-making and the wearing of festive clothes. The style in the cities is to carouse at outdoor activities or at all-night parties. In the country, however, the more traditional festivities are still popular. In Sweden, and particularly in the folklore-minded region of Dalarna, the revels focus on gaily decorated Maypoles around which the celebrants dance in rings. In Finland, sausages are barbecued on bonfires lighted to brighten the summer night.

Wearing wide-screen shades against the sun, four young women on a Stockholm street celebrate Midsummer with good-humored improvisation. Garlands of leaves and flowers are their sole gesture to tradition.

On one of the islands in the Stockholm archipelago, children and their parents prepare to dance around a Maypole to the music of a violin and an accordion. Maypoles are never erected before the eve of Midsummer Day, which is always celebrated in Sweden on the Saturday nearest to June 24.

3

Norway, destructive avalanches are generated by melting snow. In Iceland, boulders released by the thaw rattle down the scree slopes onto farmlands. In the northern cities, snow melts by day and becomes ribbed ice by night. On lakes and bays, winter roads that were marked out by stakes literally melt away, and the residents of the archipelagoes along the Gulf of Bothnia declare that spring has properly arrived when the first truck or car plunges through the ice sometime in late March or early April.

Even then, spring remains essentially a wintry season. Huge amounts of money are spent on road repairs as frost plays havoc with the foundations of roads and airport runways. And on May Day, a public holiday when graduating university students traditionally don their white caps and radicals parade with red banners, the weather is still cold enough for overcoats to be worn in most parts of Scandinavia, and the majority of trees remain bare of leaves. Only now does winter at last begin to retreat to the fells, and there it lingers in the countless deep-frozen swamps and bogs.

Given such a long and constraining winter, it is natural that the Scandinavian summer should be a cause of rhapsody. August Strindberg saw it as a season when "in all the countries of the North, the earth is a bride and the ground is full of gladness." For Danish author Johannes V. Jensen, it was "all sunshine, velvet and south wind." Of course, summer temperatures vary considerably over such a vast area, from a July mean of 51.8° F. in Reykjavik to 62.6° F. in Copenhagen, and over much of the land unseasonal frosts can still strike. But everywhere, darkness

gives way to longed-for light. Those who live within the Arctic Circle experience the nightless days of the midnight sun. Elsewhere, there are several weeks when twilight continues through the small hours, creating the so-called white nights around midsummer that are recognized as the most romantic time of year.

The responsive vegetational surge that heralds the coming of summer has to be seen to be believed. It seems almost possible to hear the plants growing. And the perfume of flowers is also unforgettable. The scent of lilac in the hedges and lily-of-the-valley in the woodlands were balm to the tormented Strindberg, as recorded in his *Diary of a Madman*. The Finnish poet Katri Vala has written about "the pagan smell of earth's skin," as yielded by the millions of acres of birches breaking into leaf and by conifers that are warmed by day and cooled by night. Icelanders know that summer has arrived when the marsh marigold and the globeflower bloom, and when cotton grass covers the swamps with a white cloak.

The great flocks of returning birds — the earliest blown in on western winds in April — is equally remarkable. Some species, to be sure, have become fewer in number than they were in the past. For example, the once-ubiquitous stork, with its twiggy nests on Jutland housetops and its beak-clapping young, finds less to feed on now that Denmark's farmers have reclaimed most of the peat bogs and drained the salt marshes where it used to flourish. But sea birds are undiminished in number. Above all, they crowd the cliffs of Iceland, the Faeroe Islands and northern Norway, and they thrive on the rich marine life of the coastal waters. Waterfowl take possession of the lakes. Wild

geese honk their way north. And after a week of warmth, clouds of midges and mosquitoes breed — to the gratification of the swifts and the swallows, but much to the discomfiture of reindeer and human alike.

The arrival of summer is accompanied by mass movement on the land. Partly to avoid the affliction of insects, domesticated herds of reindeer migrate to high altitudes or to the coastal pastures of Norway's northern seaboard. In the Baltic archipelagoes, cattle are still ferried across to traditonal grazing grounds on the many uninhabited islands. In southwest Norway, sheep are transported from the grasslands of the promontory of Jaeren to summer pastures in the highlands as much as 30 to 40 miles away. In Iceland, there is what Halldor Laxness, the Nobel prizewinning novelist, has called "a marathon of thousands of sheep" moving to "the sweets of the wilderness." In addition, wild animals emerge from winter hibernation — most notably bears, now a protected species, which roam the backwoods of Finland and northern Sweden.

By June, summer has cast its spell upon Scandinavia. Towns, parks, gardens and railroad stations are riotously red as their geraniums, petunias, salvias and cannas respond to the intense and prolonged light. Purple heather cloaks the heathlands of Jutland. The island of Gotland is distinguished by an extraordinary range of blue-flowering plants: chicory, veronicas, campanulas, pansies and the precious *Anemone pulsatila*, used as motifs on the island's tourist souvenirs. And, perhaps best of all, innumerable flowers mantle the oak and hazel glades around the margins of the Swedish and Finnish archipelagoes — the "peasants' parks," as they were named by Sweden's great botanist, Carl Linnaeus.

The time of flowers gives way to the time of fruits. Orchards and soft fruits are abundant in the principal Danish islands. Farther north, in Norway's Sogne Fjord, the raspberries — shipped by the bucketful to preserving factories — are arguably the fattest, and certainly the best flavored, in the world. The wild berry crop, too, is generous — strawberry, raspberry, gooseberry, currant, cowberry, bilberry, whortleberry, blueberry, cloudberry, rowanberry and seathorn berry. In addition there is the exotic *Rubus arcticus,* or Arctic strawberry, a berry unique to parts of Finland and Soviet Karelia, which is now an endangered species.

"My land is strawberry land: the stranger's land is bilberry land," runs a Finnish proverb, and as if to emphasize the point, the village of Suonenjoki in central Finland has its own nationally famous strawberry festival. But there the strawberries are cultivated, in contrast to the wild strawberries hallowed in the film of that name by Ingmar Bergman. In fact, the Swedish metaphor for a particularly delectable spot is *smultronställe,* a wild strawberry place. Hence, Dag Hammarskjöld, the late Swedish Secretary General of the United Nations, who was also something of a poet, summed up the essence of summer in these lines:

Midges dancing — like smoke from a furnace.
A slow-worm asleep on the footpath
To the wild strawberry place.

Just as the war on darkness and cold has imposed a distinctive wintertime life on Scandinavians, so a passion for sunshine — and for the out-of-doors — has greatly influenced the style and rhythm

Ornate wooden summer houses — one of which *(top)* is now preserved as a museum — adorn "colony gardens" in the Copenhagen suburbs. Garden plots can be bought or rented by apartment dwellers, providing a welcome escape from inner-city life and a chance to cultivate a small piece of land.

of their life in summer. Most notably, it has led to the creation of a two-house society. Many Scandinavian families now have access to a second residence in the country, which may be an elaborate villa or hunting lodge, or just a simple hut built of logs or assembled from a prefabricated kit; and most commonly, the country homes are situated near water to allow fishing or boating. (There are a quarter of a million leisure boats in Norway alone, almost one for every two families.)

In turn, a passion for sunshine has also spurred the demand for generous vacation time. On the average, Scandinavian workers have five weeks a year. Moreover, schoolchildren in all five countries have almost three full months of summer vacation, from late May to August, and it is not at all unusual for mothers and children to spend the whole period at their home in the country, perhaps being joined by fathers on the weekends.

Meanwhile, city work continues, but at the season's own leisurely pace. Summertime office hours — starting at 8 a.m. or earlier and finishing by 3 p.m. — are meant to allow workers to take maximum advantage of the long, light days. And to avoid squandering any sunshine, most workers opt for a sandwich lunch alfresco.

At the approach of Midsummer Day in late June, the great exodus from the cities begins in earnest. From now until the end of August, the chances of completing a significant business transaction are fairly negligible. Large companies operate with skeleton staffs, because large numbers of their employees, as though responding to some primeval call of the wild, have temporarily relinquished their town life for a grass-roots existence of informality border-

3

ing on downright primitivism. In the words of Danish novelist Martin A. Hansen, the Scandinavian summer is "a time of liberation through nature."

"Nature" is the key word. Whether the second homes are near sea, lake or river, in a forest or on an island, they are essentially in natural surroundings where a simplified lifestyle may be enjoyed far from the madding crowd. To be sure, some families will take along a wealth of modern gadgets: propane stoves, refrigerators, portable televisions, stereo equipment, perhaps even a radio telephone. But many others stay in homes that do not have electricity or basic services and are so far removed from civilization that only an extended journey by car or boat enables the residents to get provisions from the nearest general store.

Another popular form of escape for urbanites is the *kolonigaard,* or "colony garden," a plot of arable land on the outskirts of town. Such gardens — rented and tended by tens of thousands of Scandinavians — were originally established in Denmark in the latter part of the 19th century. Nowadays, the average *kolonigaard* measures about half an acre — a neatly maintained plot with trim surrounding hedges, fruit trees, vegetables, greenhouses and, very often, a small wooden hut for weekend habitation.

In addition to escaping to their country homes or gardens, many Scandinavians like to explore the great wilderness areas of their homelands. Many of these have been incorporated in the national parks that have burgeoned during the last generation. Norway, Sweden and Iceland all have more than one million acres reserved as national parks; Sweden also boasts nearly 2.5 million acres of protected nature preserves. Finland has a huge conservation area, which is focused on its southwest-

Aided by relatives, a farmer harvests raspberries from his land beside the Sogne Fjord in Norway. Berries have grown along the sheltered shores of the fjord since the Middle Ages, but it took modern transportation to make fruitgrowing commercially viable.

In the peaceful light of a summer's evening, fishermen try their luck on one of the tributaries of the Sogne Fjord. At least one quarter of the Norwegians are enthusiastic anglers, and virtually every child has his or her own rod.

3

ern archipelago. And in conservation-minded Denmark, where the pressures on a limited land area are so much greater, 75 wildlife preserves and about 34,500 acres of state forest preserves have been established.

Other European countries possess great nature preserves. But it is the general freedom and ease of access to the countryside that so strongly distinguish this part of the world in the summer. Campgrounds and recreational-vehicle sites abound throughout the Nordic countries. In the fells of Norway, Sweden and north Finland, long-established overnight huts are stationed at intervals along well-marked hiking trails. Be it on the broad beaches and sheltered dunes of Jutland, the pony trails of Iceland, or the totally barren and icy wastes of the east coast of Greenland (to which there are daily flights from Reykjavik), every Scandinavian can, in his or her own way, seek "liberation through nature."

Such widespread access to the land is complemented by access to the water. Most Scandinavians live within easy reach of lakes, rivers or the sea; therefore, aquatic sports — boating, water-skiing, windsurfing and swimming — are particularly popular during the summertime. None is more prevalent than fishing. It is true that some of Norway's salmon rivers have been leased for several generations to affluent foreigners; however, for the most part, fishing amenities are open to all, and amateurs far outnumber professionals in all the Nordic countries.

Nets and traps are set daily in the shallow waters near countless summer cottages, and rods and lines are stored in almost every home. Perch and pike are the principal lake fish. In the eastern interior of Finland, the lakes also

offer the delicate little *muikku,* a diminutive member of the trout family and the basis for *kalakukko,* the fish pie that is the region's speciality. Of river fish, the most common — depending on the area — are salmon, trout and whitefish, known as lavaret. Traditionally, the lavaret is smoked, whereas the salmon is more commonly salted and eaten raw.

Besides exploring their own countryside, Scandinavians also flock to the crowded tourist attractions of one another's countries. They may be drawn to the icy caverns of Norway's ancient silver mines at Kongsberg or the forestry museum beside the rushing waters of Norway's biggest river, the Lagen; to the humble surroundings of Hans Christian Andersen's birthplace in Odense or the splendors of the royal castle of Frederiksborg; to the serenities of Mårbacka, home of the well-known Swedish author Selma Lagerlöf, or the picturesque retreat of the Swedish artist Anders Zorn on Lake Silja; to Marshal Mannerheim's modest manorial birthplace at Louhisaari or the apotheosis of domestic architecture in Finland — Eliel Saarinen's home at Vitträsk, not far from Helsinki; or to Iceland's Thingvellir, site of the nation's original parliament.

Summer is also a period of wide-ranging cultural activity. Chamber-music concerts bring to life Edvard Grieg's home at Troldhaugen; intimate opera performed in Gustavus III's rococo theater at Drottningholm conjures up memories of Swedish singer Jenny Lind. Operas of a new generation of Finnish composers, such as Aulis Salonen and Joonas Kokkonen, are heard in the gaunt castle of Savonlinna; Hamlet makes regular appearances at Elsinore; and Norway's battle between hea-

then and Christian is often reenacted at Sticklestad, where Saint Olaf met his death in 1030.

Another great attraction — for Scandinavians and overseas tourists alike — is the extraordinary open-air theater of Tampere in Finland. Here, the entire auditorium — an 800-seat shell-shaped bowl — rotates to present changes of scene for the popular productions of Väinö Linna's famous epic of the Winter War, *The Unknown Soldier.* Elsewhere, outdoor theaters spring up like mushrooms (there are said to be 200 in Finland alone), and almost every district sets up its own music or folk festival, at which traditional instruments such as the Hardanger fiddle of Norway or the harplike *kantele* of Finland can be heard. And, of course, from the end of May until the beginning of September, there is Copenhagen's famous Tivoli Gardens, which can still be aptly described, in the words of the 19th-century Scandinavophile Edmund Grosse, as "the most blameless place of summer entertainment in the whole of northern Europe."

Each of the Nordic countries has its own distinct summer diversions. However, one spectacular and supremely joyful occasion is shared by all Scandinavians: the celebration of Midsummer Eve. Relic of a pagan festival that honored the longest day, Midsummer Eve is now dedicated to Saint John the Baptist, more popularly known as Saint Hans. On this liveliest night of the year, bonfires blaze splendidly beside lakes and on seashores; fireworks are set off in the dusk that precedes the dawn. Everywhere there are barbecues, and more alcohol is consumed than at any other time of the year — an excess partly explained by the fact that Midsummer is invariably the time when unem-

ployment is at its lowest and spending power at its highest.

Once upon a time, it was the custom for young women to place seven different wild flowers under their pillow on Midsummer Eve in order to encourage dreams about the man they would marry. Today, it seems, few lay their heads upon a pillow before this night of revelry has passed. But some traditions survive. Many celebrations still include old-fashioned ring dances, which involve all the company joining hands and, accompanied by concertinas, singing as they circle the embers of the bonfire. And over much of Scandinavia, the Maypole — the name comes not from the month of May but from the Old Norse verb *maja*, meaning "to adorn" — remains the colorful symbol of midsummer.

Maypoles are most spectacular in the Aland Islands, where they commonly stand as tall as masts, garlanded with leaves and flowers and crowned with ships, weathercocks, windmills and flags. They are left standing for as long as possible. Usually, however, they have become tattered by the middle of August, when Scandinavians begin holding their colorful crayfish parties. At these traditional feasts, unique to Nordic countries, mounds of the delectable little red crustaceans glow in the light of lanterns as red-bibbed, suntanned guests chase down each tail with a glass of akvavit. It is the last crayfish party — not the last rose of summer — that causes nostalgia. By then, September has arrived — time for summer homes to be shuttered against autumn gales and for the nature lovers of Scandinavia to return to their dust-sheeted homes and apartments in town and the gloomy prospect of facing another long, sun-starved winter. ☐

Children romp in a snowy school playground in the Norwegian city of Trondheim. Although the duration of snow cover around Trondheim Fjord itself is relatively short-lived, most of the country is blanketed for more than 180 days a year.

LIVING IN WINTER'S ICY GRIP

Every year, the primeval forces of winter close in on the Scandinavian countries, but they no longer bring the constraints or the real threat to survival that they inflicted upon a large part of the population for centuries. Modern technology has provided so many means of combating the effects of the cold season that the people of the far north are able to control their environment to a much greater degree than in the past.

Half a century ago, most Scandinavians were engaged in farming, forestry, fishing or mining, and the rhythm of the seasons largely controlled their activity. A short summer of intense labor for the whole family contrasted with the relative passivity and confinement of winter. Since then, industrialization has significantly reduced seasonal unemployment; and more scientific agricultural methods have led to food surpluses, thus removing the specter of winter privation. No longer are communications disrupted by snow and ice: Workers can be confident of reaching their factories and offices, and children are driven to school on time by bus.

Instead of being imprisoned by winter conditions, Scandinavians now enjoy them. Just as urban inhabitants escape to their country retreats at every available opportunity in summer, so they take with equal gusto to frozen lakes and snow-covered slopes. Winter sports are nowhere more popular than among the people of north Scandinavia. Cold-weather activities have proliferated to fill increased leisure time; in the process, a number of traditional skills that were once necessary for survival are now practiced solely for entertainment. Every winter, for example, tens of thousands of Scandinavians compete at ice fishing, in the past a vital means of obtaining winter protein. Similarly, iceboats, introduced centuries ago as emergency winter transportation, are now used strictly for pleasure.

103

Cars on a snow-plowed road in Swedish Lapland gingerly skirt loitering reindeer. Free-roaming deer and elk cause many accidents each year, and the Lapps, who own Sweden's 250,000 domesticated reindeer, receive government compensation for animals killed by motorists.

In Nordkalotten, near the Norwegian-Swedish border, wind-driven snow encrusts a road sign. Efficient snow-removal services keep all of Arctic Scandinavia's main roads and runways clear throughout the winter.

A homesteader in a remote corner of the Swedish backwoods — one of the few areas outside the national electrical grid — cuts wood for fuel. Despite the lack of electricity, he has such conveniences as a gas-powered saw, a truck and a telephone to keep in touch with the outside world.

On the frozen waters of Lake Malar, Sunday fishermen pursue the sport of ice fishing, which once helped to keep their ancestors alive through the winter. Behind them, only a few hundred yards away, the tower of Stockholm Town Hall marks the heart of the Swedish capital.

In Stockholm's Nacka park — one of several recreation areas in the city's environs — skiers pass a hardy swimmer emerging from the icy waters of a lake. Few parts of the city are out of bounds to skiers, but this area has the advantage of marked trails and floodlit skiing facilities.

On Lake Malar, competitors in an ice-boat race trim their sails to catch the breeze. Iceboats can reach speeds four times the velocity of the wind, but the sport's participants often have difficulty finding snow-free ice and favorable wind conditions at the same time.

Roaming outside a storm shelter, sheep forage through Icelandic snows to supplement their limited supplies of fodder. Iceland's sheep are too numerous for all of them to enjoy shelter in the winter; selective breeding has improved the health and strength of the stock, making them more able to survive the rigors of winter.

An international array of matchbox labels makes a colorful display at the Jonkoping Match Museum, in southern Sweden. It was at Jonkoping, in 1865, that the mechanized production of safety matches began. Sweden is the world's leading producer, with a daily output of some 50 million boxes.

A GENIUS
FOR INVENTION

A shack in the forest, a beggar's stave.
A life of poverty and a cross on the grave.

Thus a Finnish poet summed up the life of the landless peasantry in the 19th century. He was writing of his own people, but he might have been describing the plight of Scandinavians in general. At that time, little more than a century ago, the majority of the Nordic peoples were undernourished. Sweden's west-coast region of Bohuslän was described as "one great poorhouse." In Swedish Norrland, and in the backwoods of interior and northern Finland, the diet when crops failed included a bread substitute made by pulverizing the inner bark of pine trees and baking it with dried mosses and chaff.

Nor was poverty confined to the predominantly rural population. In Oslo, within a stone's throw of the royal palace, large families were living in single rooms with neither running water nor sanitation. Stockholm and Copenhagen had relatively large slum districts, and on the outskirts of Helsinki many people lived in primitive wooden shacks that were piled tightly against one another. It was a time of grave social injustice; in Sweden and Finland, farm workers still put themselves up for auction at the annual autumn labor sales, and in some areas pauper children were sold outright. It was a time, too, of widespread sickness. Although smallpox — the greatest killer in 18th-century Europe — had been virtually

conquered by the Jenner method of vaccination, tuberculosis was rife, contributing to a life expectancy throughout Scandinavia that was well below 50 years for both men and women.

"Emigrate or die" declared a Finnish newspaper headline of the 1870s. And hundreds of thousands of Scandinavians heeded such warnings by crossing the Atlantic in pursuit of a better life. Disastrous harvests from 1867 to 1869 caused an exodus of 80,000 from Sweden alone; by 1910, so many had followed that 1 in 5 Swedes lived in America. After several years, Norwegian emigration figures approached 30,000, reducing the farming populations of some areas by more than 50 percent. When the first emigrant ship sailed from Stavanger in 1825, the population of Norway was more than one million; yet within three generations it had sent three quarters of a million people on the same transatlantic voyage.

In Denmark, as in Sweden and Norway, emigration reached a high in the 1880s. In Iceland and Finland, the greatest exodus came after the turn of the century. Iceland's population of little more than 70,000 sent out at least 12,000 to the United States and to Canada, where a "New Iceland" was established on the west shore of Lake Winnipeg. By 1910, a mass migration among the rural poor had contributed 20,000 Finns to the American population. In that same year, the United States had nearly three million inhabitants who

Floating on the placid waters of Bergen harbor in western Norway, a new oil rig waits to be towed into the North Sea. By the mid-1980s, offshore oil and gas accounted for more than one third of Norway's exports and about one sixth of its gross national product.

had been born in Scandinavia, or whose parents had been born there. Most of them sought a living on the prairies of the Midwest, where they built their own cabins, often with earthen roof and walls, and only a single room to house a large family. For some, there was the discovery that they had exchanged one form of destitution for another — in America, as the Swedish author Vilhelm Moberg expressed it, "the dark is darker; the cold colder; the heat, hotter; and the mosquitoes a thousand times worse than in Sweden." For most immigrants, however, there was at least consolation in the belief that they had escaped a homeland that offered no hope for tomorrow.

They were wrong. In less than a century, Scandinavia had emerged from the economic backwoods and established itself as one of the richest regions in the world. Indeed, many Swedes, Finns, Norwegians and Danes might now argue that their home countries, not the United States, are the lands where dreams come true. As a measure of their wealth, a survey in the early 1980s showed that the national income per person in Norway was higher than in the United States and that average earnings in Sweden, Denmark and Finland were higher than in France and Britain. In almost every area of private consumption — automobiles, television sets, telephones, refrigerators, washing machines — the Nordic countries were among the leading nations, and their share of national resources allocated to public services was the highest in the world.

How was this remarkable transformation achieved? Scandinavia was not in the forefront of the Industrial Revolution; indeed, in 1900, most of the population still lived by farming, for-

estry or fishing. Nevertheless, the great economic advance can be traced to the belated arrival of industrialization after the middle of the 19th century. The European countries in which manufacturing was well established were hungry for Scandinavia's raw materials: Swedish iron ore for the furnaces of Britain and Germany; Swedish, Finnish and Norwegian timber for pit props in coal mines, sleepers for railroad tracks, telegraph poles and, above all, building construction. There was growing demand, too, for Danish dairy products and Norwegian fish to feed the urban masses of Britain and Germany. The trading boom stimulated the development of railroads and the modernization and enlargement of merchant fleets. It also encouraged the importing of new technology, which led to a dramatic expansion of the timber industry and — in Sweden especially — a thriving iron and steel industry.

Scandinavia labored under a severe handicap: It had no suitable coal reserves at a time when industrial development was basically geared to the power of the coal-fired steam engine. Norway and Sweden, with their abundance of waterfalls, were able to develop an alternative source of energy: hydroelectricity. By 1900, they derived about two thirds of their electricity from waterfalls. But even this could not compensate for the scarcity of the primary mineral of the Industrial Revolution. Indeed, from the very beginning of industrialization, the Scandinavian countries were under pressure to seek more ways of using the basic resources of their forests, farms, fisheries and mines. And this could only be done by introducing new technological processes and by devising new products.

The result validated the cliché that

necessity is the mother of invention. In seeking ways to use their resources, the Scandinavians became responsible for an astonishing array of inventions, such as the safety match, the self-aligning ball bearing, the steam turbine, the continuous milk and cream separator, the exploding harpoon gun for whaling, the first adjustable wrench and the first portable camp stove. Herein lies the key to Scandinavia's remarkable rags-to-riches progress. Other countries have responded to industrial and technological change with imagination and adaptability, but it is doubtful whether any nation of comparable size and limited resources has matched Scandinavia's record for innovation.

Among the Scandinavians, the Swedes, above all, have displayed a flair for inventiveness almost amounting to national genius. Sweden is currently registering more patents than any other country except the United States, which has a population 28 times greater. And it is a measure of the skill with which the inventions have been developed and marketed that Sweden is now the industrial giant of the North. Of the top 20 industrial enterprises in Scandinavia, 15 are Swedish, and many of the largest industries in Sweden were based on Swedish inventions and innovations.

It is not surprising that Swedish inventiveness was at first concentrated on means of using the country's two great assets: timber and iron ore. For example, G. F. Göransson, who founded a steel plant at Sandviken in 1862, was the first Scandinavian manufacturer to introduce Britain's new Bessemer steel-refining process for effective commercial exploitation. Later, around the turn of the century, a Swedish engineer, J. A. Brinell, developed a method

for determining the hardness of steel, so the Swedes were able to take a lead in producing high-quality metal for drills.

Meanwhile, the discovery of commercially viable methods of making paper from wood pulp greatly increased the demand for timber. In the 1860s, Norway had pioneered the production of mechanical pulp, which advanced the birth of the modern newspaper. A Swedish chemist, Carl Ekman, subsequently improved the process by using sulfides to dissolve lignum from wood and leave pure cellulose. In 1872, the world's first chemical pulp factory was built at Bergvik in Sweden. Not until the 1890s was the industry developed on a significant scale, but then the growth was spectacular. Between 1894 and 1914, Sweden increased production tenfold to establish itself as the world's leading exporter of mechanical and chemical pulp.

By that time, Sweden had also become the leading manufacturer of safety matches. In 1844, the safety match was invented at the Royal Caroline Institute in Stockholm by Gustav Pasch, a chemist who replaced poisonous yellow phosphorus in the match head with nontoxic amorphous phosphorus. However, the economic potential of this humble invention was not realized until after 1864, when Alexander Lagerman, a Swedish engineer, designed the first automated match machine.

In the 1920s, a single match company, Swedish Match, controlled three quarters of the world's production of matches. The company had been founded in 1917 under the presidency of Ivar Kreuger, who was the son of a match manufacturer and, according to the British economist John Maynard Keynes, the possessor of "maybe the greatest financial intelligence of his time." Kreuger's ambition was to bring all the match businesses of the world under his own control, and to achieve this aim, he offered desperately needed financial services in return for monopolistic powers. In 1927, Kreuger organized a loan of $75 million to France, and the following year, he arranged for Germany to receive a loan of $125 million. By then, Kreuger had gained control of some 250 match factories, with a

4

total output of about 30 billion boxes of matches every year.

Despite his vast resources, Kreuger was not remotely as wealthy as he made himself out to be. By juggling his holdings, inventing fictitious enterprises, forging government bonds and inflating the value of his companies, he contrived to convince the world that he was worth $400 million — in fact, the net assets of his companies were about $200 million, some $65 million less than his personal liabilities. Yet for 15 years, Kreuger beguiled the world with his outrageous financial wizardry. He visited President Hoover in the White House and Mussolini in Rome, dated Greta Garbo and kept mistresses in all the great capitals of Europe. Most remarkably, he managed to survive the great Wall Street crash of 1929.

Kreuger, Scandinavia's first world-famous industrial tycoon, liked to quote Napoleon's definition of happiness: "The ability to see difficulties gather at the same time that you can conquer them." But like Napoleon, he met his Waterloo. It came in March 1932, when he failed to negotiate loans needed to meet his multimillion-dollar debts. Recognizing that financial disaster was imminent, he entertained his young Finnish mistress at his Paris apartment; the next day, he shot himself. In Sweden, there was a day of mourning. Flags were flown at half-mast. Politicians paid their tributes. And later, thousands lined the route of his funeral procession in Stockholm.

Soon afterward, an official examination of the Kreuger empire revealed that he had "grossly misrepresented the true financial position." But it was to take five years of investigation into 400 companies before the true enormity of this misrepresentation could be

An agile tug crewman vaults to check the bindings on a consignment of logs being towed from the forested center of Finland to paper mills in the south. Lumber is the mainstay of the Finnish economy: Timber-based products make up about one third of the nation's exports.

4

appreciated. In the process, 20 directors and accountants were brought to trial and jailed. A newspaper headline proclaimed sadly: "The Collapse of Sweden's Second Empire." John Kenneth Galbraith, the American economist, subsequently described Kreuger as "by all odds, the biggest thief in the history of larceny." Yet, remarkably, it was not the end of Kreuger's Swedish Match. Although its debts exceeded $28 million, Swedish financiers recognized it as a basically sound business that could be salvaged. Sixteen years later, the company was finally able to pay dividends on its shares.

Today, Swedish Match is a solid and respectable group, still the largest producer of matches in the world. But the "little wooden soldiers," as Kreuger used to call his matches, only account for about one quarter of the company's business. The bulk of its profits are derived from an enormous variety of other wood and paper products. In this respect, the progress of Swedish Match is a typical Swedish success story: a company that started out by exploiting a single invention and then diversified.

Many of Sweden's other great international companies owe their existence to inventions made by Swedish engineers decades ago. They include ASEA, the huge electrical engineering and electronics group founded in 1883 to manufacture the generators invented by Jonas Wenström; the Ericsson group, a telecommunications giant whose founder patented the first desk telephone to combine mouthpiece and receiver in one unit; the Facit Group, a major office-equipment and computer manufacturer that grew out of Willgodt Odhner's invention in 1874 of the world's first practical adding machine; and SKF, which was founded in 1907

on Sven Wingquist's invention of the self-aligning ball bearing and is now the world's leading manufacturer of bearings, producing 25,000 varieties, from the size of a pinhead to giants weighing up to three tons.

In some cases, inventions dramatically transformed companies that were already established. A classic example was the Swedish firm of AGA, founded in 1904 for the production of liquid acetylene gas. Gustaf Dalén joined the company as chief engineer, and thereafter, its future was inextricably linked to his inventions. One of his most novel ideas was the AGA sun valve, a solar-operated switch for turning lighthouse beacons on at dark and off at daybreak. Despite derisive reaction from other scientists and from patent offices, his invention worked. Fifty years after it was marketed, there were more than 25,000 solar-operated AGA beacons lighting the sea lanes of the world — some of them having operated without repair for half a century.

By a tragic irony, the man who brought light into darkness was blinded when he was drenched in flaming acetylene during an experiment. His brother, a renowned eye surgeon, tried vainly to restore Dalén's vision. Yet, even without his sight, Dalén continued his innovative work for another quarter of a century. He carried out research into radio communications that was to pave the way for transistors, television sets and stereophonic sound systems; and it was during his years of blindness that he devised the fuel-efficient stove that has become synonymous with his company's name.

Another Swedish group whose products are sold worldwide is Alfa-Laval. The company was founded by Gustav de Laval, an engineer and chemist who

revolutionized dairy farming by his invention, in 1878, of a continuous centrifugal milk and cream separator. This simple invention, which almost every farmer could afford to buy, was especially valuable to the agriculture-based economy of Denmark. And as the company's production advanced, more and more applications were discovered for the invention, which could be used to purify, clarify and concentrate all manner of substances: food, fuel, chemicals, pharmaceuticals.

In all, Laval had 92 patents to his credit. They covered, among other things, a milking machine, the application of the rotation principle for the mass production of glass bottles and, most important, the invention of the steam turbine in 1893. Yet Laval was by no means the most prolific Swedish inventor. He was eclipsed by a contemporary, Alfred Nobel, who held more than 350 Swedish and foreign patents. Paradoxically, Nobel, who developed new explosives and made a personal fortune from armaments, is now best known to the world as a philanthropic pacifist. Nobel bequeathed 33 million kronor to an investment trust, its earnings to be "annually distributed in the form of prizes to those who have conferred the greatest benefit on mankind."

Alfred Nobel was born in Stockholm in 1833, the son of an enterprising engineer-inventor who built steamships and submarine mines for tsarist Russia. In 1859, the family business went bankrupt and Alfred came to the rescue by patenting a detonator for use with nitroglycerine. The invention engendered the first of his fortunes at a time when the building of railways, roads and tunnels had made blasting a big business. Indirectly, it also led to the

THE BEQUEST OF A DANISH BREWER

Internationally, the name of Carlsberg — Denmark's largest brewer — is synonymous with beer, the product it exports to some 130 countries. Danes, however, know the firm as the sponsor of the Carlsberg Foundation, a philanthropic institution that devotes its profits — approximately five million dollars in 1985 — to the advancement of human knowledge and understanding.

The man responsible for initiating such magnanimity was the company's founder, J. C. Jacobsen. A fervent patriot, he set up the Carlsberg Foundation in 1876 to support scientific research. Thirty years later, his son Carl widened the scope of the policy to include the arts and humanities. Since then, the foundation has sent expeditions to the Arctic, financed research into cancer and the atom, restored national buildings, created the Glyptotek, Copenhagen's great art museum, and commissioned works of art.

Not the least of Jacobsen's bequests to the nation was his sumptuous residence in the capital. According to his wishes, it serves as a Mansion of Honor, to be occupied for life by a distinguished Dane. Its four residents to date have included Nobel prize-winning nuclear physicist Neils Bohr.

Modern technology aids the traditional process of brewing in copper vats.

A Carlsberg dray passes the factory gates.

Crates of empty bottles lie ready for refilling at the company's plant in Copenhagen.

A worker maneuvers sides of pork at a meat-processing plant in Vejle, in eastern Jutland. Beginning in the early 1950s, the pig population of Denmark rose steadily and by the mid-1980s was approaching 10 million.

growth of his reputation as a "mad scientist" and a "merchant of death."

On September 3, 1864, the Nobel workshop at Heleneborg, on the outskirts of Stockholm, blew up, killing Alfred's younger brother, a mechanic, a boy assistant, a maid and a passing workman. Banished from the city, Nobel resumed production aboard a hired barge on Lake Malar and later established an explosives factory in Hamburg, Germany. But then news came of another disaster. Off Aspinwall (later renamed Colón), on the Atlantic coast of Panama, a steamer carrying a cargo of nitroglycerine exploded, with the loss of 74 lives. Fourteen people died when another consignment shattered the San Francisco warehouse of Wells Fargo and Co. Across the world in Sydney, a warehouse and adjoining houses were razed. Then Nobel's own factory in Hamburg was destroyed.

Public alarm turned to panic, with some countries restricting the shipment of nitroglycerine and some banning it altogether. Nobel set to work, seeking a way to minimize the dangers of handling the notoriously unstable liquid. His search ended in 1867, when he found that mixing nitroglycerine with a kind of fine clay produced a substance that could be dropped, shaken, heated and hammered without exploding. He called his invention "dynamite." Before long, his discovery was in demand worldwide. It was used to blast out the Simplon Tunnel between Italy and Switzerland and to excavate the Panama Canal; it thundered ahead of every railroad construction gang from Sweden to Japan.

Nobel went to build up a great armaments empire. Optimistically, in a letter to Baroness Bertha von Suttner, a leading campaigner for world peace, he wrote: "My factories may make an end of war sooner than your congresses. The day when two army corps can annihilate each other in seconds, all civilized nations, it is to be hoped, will recoil from war and discharge their troops." Perhaps it was just as well that he did not live to see the destruction wreaked by his weapons in World War I.

At the dawn of Scandinavia's industrial revolution, Norway, like Sweden, benefited greatly from the new processes for mineral and paper production. But, above all, Norway benefited from the development of hydroelectric power, popularly known as "white coal." The potential for such development was enormous in a country that has a very high level of precipitation (as much as 78 inches a year in some areas) and hundreds of towering waterfalls. Toward the realization of this potential, 11 hydroelectronic plants were built between 1896 and 1900, and by the turn of the century, industry was using three times as much horsepower from electricity as from steam engines.

Norway, however, had even fewer industrial raw materials than Sweden, and so the problem was to find productive outlets for such an abundance of energy. Norwegian innovation came to the rescue by creating an entirely new industry: the manufacture of synthetic fertilizers. Two Norwegians, Professor Kristian Birkeland, an academic physicist, and Samuel Eyde, an industrial engineer, devised a means of using electrical energy to extract nitrogen from the atmosphere; and, in 1905, the commercial exploitation of their technique resulted in the foundation of Norsk Hydro, which became Norway's biggest industrial concern. Norsk Hydro remains Norway's largest company and still produces synthetic fertilizers, although these are now based on petroleum rather than nitrogen. Surplus electrical power is used in the making of a large range of other products, from aluminum and magnesium to furniture and packaging materials.

As a result of its hydroelectric resources, Norway now produces more electricity per capita than any other country in the world. Its output is almost twice that of its nearest rivals, Canada and the United States. Largely on the strength of this resource, Norway has advanced from being one of Western Europe's poorest countries to one of its richest. In 1970, even before the profits from North Sea oil began to pour in, Norway was among the top 10 countries in the world with regard to gross national product on a per capita basis. Yet the nation could not have so rapidly capitalized on her "white-coal" potential had it not been for the earnings generated by her traditional merchant marine and fishing enterprises.

In 1900, Norway's merchant fleet was the third largest in the world, and there were more Norwegians engaged in fishing and whaling than in industry. Here again, inventiveness played an important part. In 1864, for example, a Norwegian fisherman, Svend Foyn, revolutionized whaling by developing a gun to fire harpoons with explosive heads. The gun was so effective that he killed 32 blue whales on one expedition, whereas on a previous trip, using a conventional harpoon, he had caught only one whale. Thereafter, Norwegian whalers began to venture farther afield, spending entire Antarctic summers in the waters around the South Pole icecap, where finback whales were to be found in large numbers.

Increased catches spurred other in-

novations. In 1905, the first floating factory whaler was launched from a Norwegian dock; and in 1924, a Norwegian whale gunner devised a special kind of slipway for hauling whales onto the deck of a factory ship, where they could be flensed and prepared for boiling. Between 1927 and 1931, the total output of Antarctic whale oil more than quadrupled, with Norway taking two thirds of the world harvest.

In 1969, in the face of worldwide concern about declining whale populations, Norway retired most of its whaling fleet. In other respects, however, Norwegian fishing boats continue to gather a valuable harvest from the sea. In 1914, fishing provided 50,000 Nor-

wegians with their primary source of income, and approximately 90 percent of Norway's fish catch was exported. Today there are still some 35,000 professional fishermen in Norway — far more than the combined totals of all the other Scandinavian countries — and 90 percent of the catch (slightly less than three million tons a year) is sold abroad, making Norway the largest exporter of fish and fish products in Europe.

The extent of this surplus reflects both the richness of Norway's fishing grounds and the ingenuity of its fishermen. In the 1870s, the opening of a canning factory at Stavanger ushered in the age of the canned sardine. Norway was one of the first countries to

produce a professional class of fishermen operating decked, deep-sea boats equipped with cable-strengthened nets; it was also one of the first to introduce carrier vessels to transport freshly caught fish to the coastal processing plants, allowing the fleets to remain in continuous operation at sea. At the same time, Norway led the way with large-scale refrigeration (there are some 230 freezing plants along the Norwegian coast, and each year between 10 and 12 percent of Norway's total catch is frozen).

Another major innovation since the early 1960s has been the establishment of fish farms, which are now operating in hundreds of sheltered bays, fjords

Sightseers stroll past a model of Amalienborg Palace, residence of the Danish royal family.

Hans Andersen assumes a new dimension.

In this replica of a Copenhagen harbor area, no building is more than four feet tall.

A WORLDWIDE BUSINESS BUILT ON TOY BRICKS

In 1932, Ole Kirk Christiansen, a carpenter from the Jutland village of Billund, started making wood toys to supplement his income. The firm he founded — Lego, from the Danish *leg godt*, or "play well" — became a gold mine 25 years later, when his son introduced a new line: interlocking bricks that could be shaped into almost any form a child could imagine. The response was immediate, and Lego became a multimillion-dollar enterprise, with more than 50,000 retail outlets worldwide.

The most spectacular display of Lego's achievements can be seen in Billund. There, on a 25-acre site, the company has created the miniature world of Legoland Park. Made up of more than 30 million bricks forming models that range from replicas of spacecraft to Copenhagen landmarks, the park has become Denmark's biggest tourist attraction outside the capital.

Legoland provides its own model of the famous bronze statue of the Little Mermaid.

and skerries bordering the Atlantic. By the mid-1980s, the bulk of Norway's salmon and trout — about 22,300 tons a year — came from private net-enclosed reserves, where the fish are scientifically spawned and fed on a diet provided by the ocean. In these protected conditions, salmon reach an average weight of nine pounds in two years. Immediately after harvesting, a large proportion of the crop is exported by air, in specially designed refrigerated containers, to more than 20 countries, including the United States and Japan.

Norway's other traditional maritime strength is its merchant navy — until 1976, the fourth largest in the world with a gross registered tonnage of 26.8 million. Until the late 1970s, Norway's 200 shipping companies prospered by operating custom-built cargo vessels and oil tankers. Most of these ships were designed for specific tasks and manned by specialized crews; and they were the most up-to-date in the world because they were replaced by new models on an average of every six years, compared with a world average of 11 years. However, one feature of Norway's specialization almost proved to be its undoing. In 1973, when the energy crisis broke on an unsuspecting world, 20 million tons of Norwegian shipping was in oil tankers, including 72 tankers of more than 100,000 tons — far too many for the reduced amount of oil available. Many tankers had to be laid up: 100 vessels were idle in 1976, and although the number of out-of-service ships decreased to 44 in 1978, the continuing recession and competition from other shipbuilding nations saw the Norwegian merchant marine steadily fall to seventh position in the world.

It was, therefore, ironic that oil and natural gas should also prove Norway's greatest economic blessing. The first discoveries in the Norwegian sector of the North Sea were made in 1969 and 1970. No one knows with certainty the amount of oil and gas that exists in the Norwegian fields, but estimates indicate total reserves of four to five billion tons. By the mid-1980s, production had risen to more than 50 million tons a year. Since Norway's own annual demand was less than nine million tons, the country had a huge surplus for export — the equivalent of the combined needs of Sweden and Denmark. And the income earned from this oil bonanza had raised Norway in the ratings of wealthy nations from ninth place in the early 1970s to a position of vying with Switzerland for the highest standard of living in the world.

In the late 19th century, when neighboring Sweden and Norway were in the throes of economic change, Iceland was still locked into a preindustrial structure that was as primitive as it was poor. In 1900, there was not a factory in the country; there were scarcely any passable roads, no bridges, no artificial harbors and few stone houses. The people remained dependent on the resources of the sea and animal husbandry.

The first sign of industrialization in Iceland was the adaptation of the fishing fleet from open rowboats to decked vessels that were capable of venturing to distant waters. The founding of a national bank and the progress of the cooperative movement, which was established in 1882, also promised the Icelanders better trading opportunities. In the 20th century, the size of their catches — mainly herring, cod and haddock — steadily mounted as a result of more sophisticated techniques, the introduction of superefficient, large-decked stern trawlers, and the development of fishing as a year-round activity instead of a seasonal one.

Because fishing was so critical to its economy and because it feared exploitation of nearby fishing grounds by foreign fleets, Iceland unilaterally extended its fishing limits — from four to 12 miles in 1958, then to 50 miles in 1971, and 200 miles in 1975. These actions led to the so-called Cod Wars: *opéra bouffe* affairs that consisted of a series of minor skirmishes between Icelandic coastguard cutters and British trawlers and frigates, but that escalated to the point of causing casualties. In 1974, the U.N.'s International Court of Justice at The Hague ruled against Iceland, but world opinion and political considerations persuaded Britain to concede to its tiny NATO ally in 1976.

Victory in this matter, however, did not bring the expected gains. Cod stocks continued to diminish, possibly because of climatic changes or perhaps due to new patterns in the movement of fish. Whatever the cause, Iceland was compelled to develop its economy in other directions — to such effect that manufacturing and services now claim a majority of the employed population. Industries, mostly small in scale, range from dairying and meat production to greenhouse cultivation and knitwear. But there are few large-scale enterprises, mainly because the domestic market is too small to support major industries and the international market too distant to allow profitable trade.

Yet Iceland does have enormous potential wealth in its abundance of hydroelectric resources and geothermal energy from its hot springs. As an Icelandic minister of industry stressed not long ago: "Our oil is flowing all over the country — in our rivers, in our water-falls, and under the ground." This "oil" cannot be put in barrels and shipped overseas. However, it has been suggested that the process might work in reverse: that foreign companies might bring their plants to the energy source. In theory, this could be achieved. In practice, it is unlikely, because of the small size of the domestic market and the high transportation costs from such an isolated island. Until this problem can be solved, Iceland's economy must remain largely dependent on the products of its farms and fisheries.

Finland, like Iceland, lagged behind the rest of Scandinavia in moving toward industrialization until after World War II. To a degree, the Finns were held back by lack of capital investment in the late 19th century and then by the struggle for independence from Russia. More generally, however, their slow development was due to the nature of their land (roughly 80 percent forest and water), together with their harsh climate and remote location. In 1917, when Finland became an independent republic, some 70 percent of the population was still employed in agriculture and forestry; and for most Finns, the new technology of the industrial age simply meant more varied and more economical means of processing forest and farm products.

When the country eventually began to industrialize on a broad front, it changed from an agrarian to an urban society at an astonishing rate. In 1950, 50 percent of the gainfully employed population derived a living from the land; by the mid-1980s, about 10 percent did. In common with all the Scandinavian states, Finland now has an economy in which service industries and commerce dominate the employ-ment structure. Metallurgical and engineering industries employ a larger percentage of the work force than forest-based ones; and well-known exports of textiles, clothing, ski equipment (Finland is the world's largest manufacturer) and domestic goods are of modest consequence beside lesser known exports of major capital goods.

Finland has competed successfully in Latin America, Africa, the Middle East and Southeast Asia for the sale of entire papermaking, hydroelectric power and metallurgical plants. Unlike the other Scandinavian nations, it has also developed an important market in the Soviet Union. For a generation, the Soviets have been buying Finnish-made icebreakers, lake and river craft, as well as floating dormitories for construction workers. The largest single enterprise conducted across Finland's eastern border has been the construction of a huge iron and steel complex at Kostamus in the Karelian Soviet Republic. When this was under way in the 1970s, it provided as many jobs for commuting Finnish workers as the entire North Sea oil industry did for Norwegians.

These achievements have been accomplished despite the fact that Finland has limited resources and has to import nearly two thirds of its energy needs. They seem even more impressive given that Finland's 1941 to 1944 war with the Soviet Union cost the country enormous reparations and 10 percent of her territory, including a part of Lapland rich in nickel deposits. Those reparations, payable over eight years, took the form of ships, locomotives, machinery, electrical equipment, building components and even complete industrial plants. At that time, Finland had only a few, modest-sized heavy engineering and metal indus-

An icebreaker plowing through the frozen waters of the Baltic testifies to the engineering skill of Finland's shipbuilders. Pioneers in Arctic technology, the Finns have designed a nuclear-powered icebreaker.

tries, and a limited number of trained engineers and skilled technicians.

Ironically, these enforced payments were to prove just the economic stimulus that Finland needed. They compelled the nation to develop a broader industrial base on which to build for the future. As Finnish observers noted at the time, that base had balanced too long on a single wooden leg; now they were gaining a second leg of metal. It soon emerged that there were other possibilities for the new industries to exploit. Geological exploration revealed that Finland's mineral resources, though limited, were reasonably varied and could be mined: pyrites, iron ore, zinc and modest quantities of various other minerals. In the early 1970s, the products of the metal and engineering industries accounted for more than 25 percent of Finnish export, and Finland had become one of the world's largest producers of vanadium, used to manufacture steel.

As did Germany after World War II, Finland profited in the long run from being forced to build new industries from the ground up, without the burden of antiquated machinery and methods. For example, the nation had to cede its entire fleet of icebreakers as reparations. In the course of replacing these vital components of the merchant marine, Finnish engineers developed an unrivaled expertise in icebreaker construction, pioneering the use of propellers at both ends of the ship, twin rudders, and a hull designed to withstand pressures many times greater than conventional designs.

As a result, the country emerged as a world leader in icebreaker technology. By the mid-1980s, the Wärtsila shipyards of Helsinki and Turku had built 60 percent of all the world's icebreakers

constructed since World War II and had captured 30 percent of the world's cruise-ship market. Wärtsila also led in Arctic offshore technology, and its research equipment now includes the world's largest laboratory for the testing of model ships designed to sail in frozen waters. In this laboratory, a 230-foot-long tank can simulate all kinds of ice conditions, with video cameras recording the interaction of ice and propellers, rudders and hulls. Wärtsila's experience and experimental facilities have been called upon by other countries — especially, Canada, the United States and the U.S.S.R. — which are concerned with sailing in ice-clogged waters. Finnish technology is likely to be of considerable significance for the commerical exploitation of oil fields hidden under the polar ice.

Despite these diverse industrial developments, Finland's great forests remain the backbone of the economy. New technologies have transformed the physical management of the forests and, at the same time, dramatically expanded the range of products to be derived from timber. Until the late 19th century, the logger with an ax exploited timber almost as a wild crop. Since the 1950s — by which time Finland's forested area had been surveyed in detail and brought within the zone of commercial exploitation — timber has been treated as a rotation crop, felled by power saw, and carefully nurtured by seed-breeding, draining, planting, fertilizing and selective harvesting. As a result, the consumption of timber by industry has doubled in one generation without depleting the forest.

An ever-increasing number of mechanical processes has diversified the output of forest products, ranging from deal board and plywood to wall-

board and laminates, from prefabricated houses and saunas to hundreds of different kinds of paper and, not least, to dozens of chemicals produced as byproducts through fermentation and distillation. In the mid-1980s, Finnish pulp and paper goods made up more than 60 percent of its forest products, and the vast bulk was exported, satisfying nearly one quarter of Europe's demand. *The Times* and the *Daily Mail* of London and *Le Monde* and *Le Figaro* of Paris are among the many foreign publications printed on Finnish paper. Forest industries continue to account for about one third of export earnings and are more important to Finland than to any other Scandinavian country.

Although Finland and Iceland were late to industrialize, they did at least have vast resources of timber and geothermal power. Denmark, in contrast, was unique among Scandinavian countries in lacking large forests and being virtually devoid of metals, coal and other energy sources. Thus, while Sweden and Norway were engaged in industrial transformation, Denmark's attention was focused on agriculture, which had to be modernized and greatly expanded if the country was to balance its exports with its import needs.

This was a daunting challenge for two reasons. First, Denmark had lost two fifths of her territory — much of it good farmland — in the 1864 war with Germany. Second, her traditional grain crops could no longer compete with the cheap American imports that flooded into Western Europe after the transcontinental railroads had opened trade routes to the Atlantic ports.

Denmark's loss of farmland was offset partly by the activities of a young road engineer, Enrico Dalgas, who, in

A worker puts the finishing touches on an industrial robot manufactured by a Swedish engineering and electronics enterprise. In the mid-1980s, there were 30 robots for every 10,000 workers in Swedish industry — the highest ratio in the world.

1866, inspired the foundation of the Danish Heath Society to promote land reclamation, particularly in Jutland. By carefully tilling the sandy soils, draining the peat bogs, introducing root crops to rotation farming and planting coniferous shelter belts, the Danes brought hitherto unproductive areas into cultivation. By 1914, the addition to the cultivated area in Jutland alone had compensated for what had been lost to Germany. Meanwhile, the problem of American grain imports was overcome by a dramatic switch from arable to animal products.

The move began in the 1870s. Within little more than a decade, animal husbandry had reached such a scale that Danish farmers were exporting to Britain's industrial cities substantial quantities of dairy products and bacon, shipped by way of the newly created North Seaport of Esbjerg. By the end of the 19th century, Denmark was the world's largest exporter of these products. Critical to this achievement was the development of cooperative processing and marketing organizations, which ensured that the products were of standard types and that qualities were carefully adapted to the demands of different markets. The first cooperative dairy was founded by the farmers of West Jutland in 1882; in less than a decade, there were 700 and, by the turn of the century, more than 1,000.

Farmers are notoriously conservative, and it is unlikely that the rise of rural cooperatives would have been so quick and effective if the way had not been prepared through a unique educational plan, initiated in the 1840s by Bishop N.F.S. Grundtvig. A patriotic idealist, Grundtvig was determined to improve educational standards among the rising generation of country folk.

He achieved this by founding residential establishments, known as folk high schools, for young adult members of the farming community. It was a measure of his achievement that by 1900, some 15 percent of the students at folk high schools were from families that owned small farms, and his educational scheme had been adopted by other Scandinavian countries. Meanwhile, the cooperative movement had taken hold in Norway, Sweden and Iceland, and it was spreading farther: Shortly before World War I, Finland was to be dubbed "a nation of cooperators" by Swedish economist Thorsten Odhe. In more recent years, even the Lapps have followed Denmark's lead by establishing a cooperative factory for processing reindeer products.

As Scandinavia's most cultivable country, Denmark remained a predominantly agricultural land well into the 20th century. As late as the 1950s, farm products accounted for more than 50 percent of Danish exports. However, the Danes used the healthy profits generated by their food exports to develop both light and heavy industries. In the latter half of the 19th century, Danish entrepreneur T. F. Tietgen founded a telegraph company and a shipping company. He also expanded the engineering firm of Burmeister and Wain, which built the first diesel-powered ship in 1912. Burmeister and Wain is now the world's biggest manufacturer of diesel engines.

It was hardly an industrial advance to match that of neighboring Sweden. But then, after World War II, an injection of much-needed capital investment, via the United States' Marshall Plan, launched Denmark into a second industrial revolution. By the mid-1950s, manufacturing capacity equaled that of agriculture; today, industry accounts for some 70 percent of Denmark's exports, compared with agriculture's 30 percent. With fewer workers and increasing mechanization and specialization, the productivity of farms has increased to such a degree that one farm worker now produces enough food for 100 people, compared with 35 in 1950; and about two thirds of agricultural

MASTERWORKS OF SCANDINAVIAN DESIGN

production can be exported. Related to this achievement has been the production of agricultural equipment — small harvesters, tractors and other machines — scaled down to suit the size of Denmark's small farms and the size of the farmer's pocketbook.

Undoubtedly, the strongest commercial resource possessed by the Danes is their native wit and intelligence. These qualities have enabled them to work their own kind of economic miracle. They are almost entirely beholden to overseas suppliers for their raw materials, and yet a veritable flood of products has poured into the export market from Danish factories, workshops and shipyards — everything from fiberglass sailing dinghies to 500,000-ton supertankers; from nail polish to special cements for use in extreme climatic conditions; from pharmaceuticals (Denmark is the world's major manufacturer of insulin) to resuscitation equipment; from experimental plastic balls designed for raising sunken ships to automatically operated bridges and desalinization plants; from silverware and porcelain to every conceivable item for furnishing the home and clothing the body.

Danish electronic equipment has been landed on the moon. Many countries use its X-ray equipment to test seam welds on aircraft hulls. Danish building systems are bought by nations that wish to revive housing shortages quickly and efficiently. Through experience in linking together the islands of their fragmented country, Danish engineers have established an international reputation for bridge building and harbor construction. And parents all over the world who want to amuse and educate their children at the same time give them Lego bricks, which were devised

From the 1930s through the 1950s and 1960s, the bold modernity of Scandinavian-made ceramics, glassware, fabrics and furniture transformed the look of home and office furnishings around the world. The hallmarks of visual grace, simplicity and craftsmanship that characterized Scandinavian design had their roots in a long tradition of Viking and folk art. The immediate inspiration, however, was the concept of functional design formulated in the 1930s by the German Bauhaus school of artist-craftsmen, and reflected by Nordic designers who were aware of the need to bring beauty and style to mass-produced goods. The key elements of functionalism — simple construction techniques, clean lines and natural materials — were applied to almost every conceivable type of artifact,

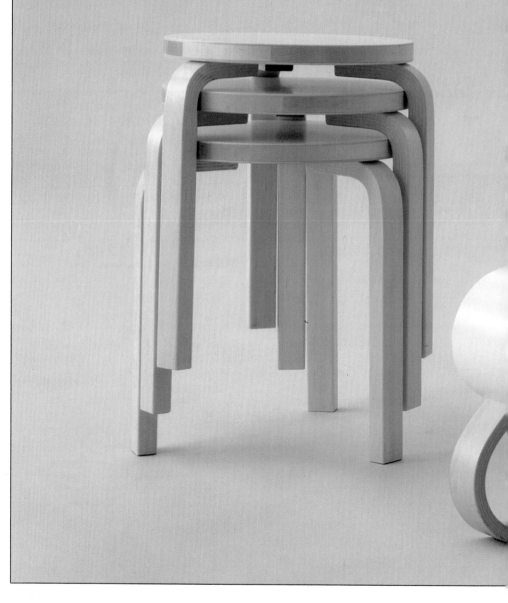

but were most effective in the design of seating. Without sacrificing comfort, the chair was stripped of upholstery and ornamentation in the now-classic plywood and laminated bentwood model *(below, right)*, produced by the Finnish architect Alvar Aalto for the Paimio sanatorium in 1930. Six years later, he showed the same practical approach in devising easily stacked stools for libraries *(below, left)*.

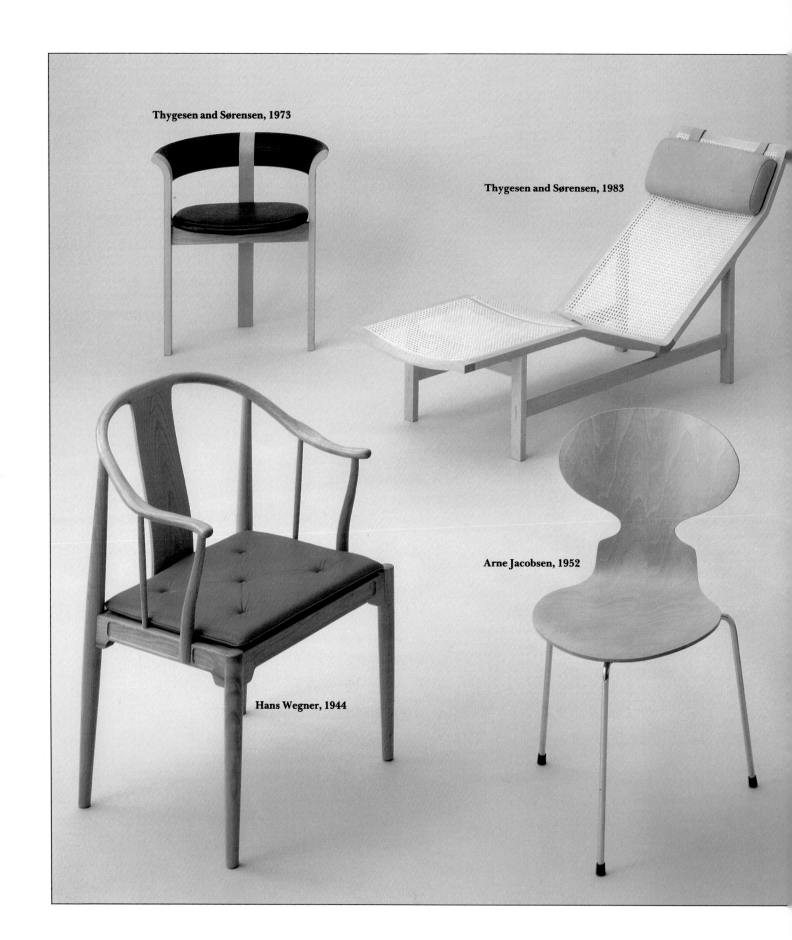

Thygesen and Sørensen, 1973

Thygesen and Sørensen, 1983

Arne Jacobsen, 1952

Hans Wegner, 1944

Mogens Koch, 1932

Although they were designed over a period of 50 years, the classic Danish chairs shown here share the elements of simplicity and streamlined elegance. Beech is the wood most commonly used; other materials range from the cherry wood chosen for Hans Wegner's Chinese Chair to the cane, leather and stainless steel of Poul Kjaerholm's Hammock.

Hvidt and Mølgaard-Nielsen, 1960

Poul Kjaerholm, 1965

4

in the 1950s by the ingenious son of a Jutland carpenter and which are now a multimillion-dollar business.

The success story of Denmark's manufacturing industries reflects an attitude shared by Scandinavia as a whole. The Nordic countries recognized that, with limited raw materials and high labor costs, they would have difficulty in producing competitively priced goods for export. Independently, they arrived at the conclusion that if they could not compete on basic price, they must offer superior value for the money. One way was to build a reputation for goods of durability and reliability — those qualities embodied in the utilitarian solid-fuel stove that Gustaf Dalén had made virtually indestructible and so efficient that it could be kept burning for up to 24 hours without refueling.

Dalén's stove, still widely used in Europe, is obviously the work of a practical engineer, not a design department. The same is true of Sweden's Volvo and Saab vehicles. Volvos have the enviable reputation of being the world's most durable mass-produced cars, with a life expectancy of more than 20 years. Saabs, too, have a reputation for reliability that is enhanced by their success in auto rallies. Moreover, both cars are technically innovative. Volvo pioneered many of the safety features now built into competitors' vehicles, and Saab was the first to market a turbo-powered sedan that increased performance without affecting economy.

Another factor in Scandinavia's commercial success has been design. Beginning in the 1920s with the German-inspired movement for "beautiful things for everyday use," Scandinavian manufacturers have been associated with clean, smooth lines in furniture, colorful and practical kitchenware, and streamlined household accessories. In that decade, the need for things stylish but simple was advocated by Poul Henningsen, a Danish architect, designer and creator of ingenious lampshades. "Throw away your artists' berets and bow ties and get into overalls," he exhorted his colleagues. "Down with artistic pretentiousness. Simply make things that are fit for use: That is enough to keep you busy, and you will sell vast quantities and make lots of money."

It so happened that Scandinavian designers were in a better position than their foreign rivals to heed such advice. A native craft tradition had been kept alive through the 19th century by various national societies, including the Swedish Society of Industrial Design, founded in 1845. This was the first of its kind in the world; it was followed 30 years later by the Finnish Society of Crafts and Design. Furthermore, the late arrival of the industrial revolution in Scandinavia meant that many small folk-art enterprises flourished alongside mass-production factories well into the 20th century, so providing a source of inspiration to designers when public taste began to rebel against the domestic goods then available.

The Danes and the Finns led the way. Their influence was most evident in the works of the Finnish architect Alvar Aalto and his Danish contemporary Arne Jacobsen, who was instrumental in popularizing the elegant light furnishings that, by the late 1930s, were to be seen in many Scandinavian homes. After World War II, the Danes in particular gave a distinctive and attractive look to the products of high technology as much as to the traditional craft industries. Emphasis on original design led to a profitable expansion of Danish silver and porcelain, and before long, a reputation for original styling had been won for Norwegian enameling, Swedish glass, Finnish furniture and Icelandic woolens. By then, the term "Scandinavian Design" had come to represent distinctive and uniform quality, because the Nordic countries had developed their creative styles on similar lines and there had been considerable cross-fertilization.

The designers themselves brought the Scandinavian touch to overseas countries. Finnish architect Eliel Saarinen led the way by influencing the development of the American skyscraper; his son Eero was the architect for the U.S. Embassy in London. Another Finnish architect, Wiljo Rewell, gave Toronto its City Hall. Alvar Aalto was responsible for distinctive buildings in the United States, Germany, Italy and many other European countries. Arne Jacobsen designed St. Catherine's College, Oxford, and left his mark in such faraway places as Hawaii, Peru and Zambia, where his furniture was used in churches, hospitals, hotels, offices, town halls and universities. And in the 1950s, a young Danish architect, Joern Utzon, won an international design competition for the Sydney Opera House, an architectural masterpiece that ultimately cost $104 million.

For all its originality and practicality, Scandinavian design has now probably passed the zenith of its influence. There is a saturation point in most styles, and as European homes and European tastes grow increasingly standardized, the scope for variety, particularly in the simple Scandinavian style, diminishes all the time. In fact, the emphasis in the design field has now moved away from domestic products toward the area of high technology —

advanced instruments, electronics, robotics, telecommunications, chemicals and pharmaceuticals.

Today, Scandinavian industry has entered a new era of international trade in which multinational companies, such as Ericsson, ASEA and Electrolux, are extending their bases overseas by buying up existing companies or selling to markets as distant as Japan, Brazil or India. At the same time, there is more emphasis on marketing the accumulated expertise of high-tech industries — for example, the know-how to build and operate softwood processing plants, hydroelectric power stations and cement-manufacturing plants. A senior executive of Alfa-Laval explains, "We have shifted from selling components to selling entire systems and the knowledge of how to make the best use of those systems." Such ambitious international marketing — practiced to a greater or lesser degree by Sweden, Denmark, Finland and Norway — is certainly a far cry from the years, a century ago, when Scandinavia's contribution to the world was its poor and its dispossessed citizens.

Lecturing to students in Helsinki in 1867, Zachris Topelius summed up the three keys to history: geographical position, natural conditions and the ability of people to use them. With its northerly location and limited resources, Scandinavia was certainly not favored in the first two respects. But the challenge its hardships and handicaps presented greatly spurred ingenuity, enterprise and industry. It has been the ability of the Nordic peoples to explore and exploit the unpromising hand dealt by nature that has made, if not quite a paradise, a society of material comfort and security out of land that was once largely a forbidding wilderness. □

A pair of sculpted figures serve as lamp standards above the main entrance to the Helsinki railroad station. Designed by Finnish architect Eliel Saarinen and completed in 1914, the station is an early example of the Scandinavian flair for combining the functional with the ornamental.

134

AN IMAGINATIVE CONCERN FOR YOUNG CHILDREN

Few nations are as well provided with leisure facilities for their children as the Scandinavian lands. Recreation areas furnished with play equipment, usually made of plastic or wood and designed to be both safe and good-looking, can be found in almost all town centers, many large department stores and even on ferries. Public libraries have juvenile sections that often lend toys, games and records as well as books. Such facilities for fun reflect the emphasis that Scandinavian governments place on the welfare of children.

There are pressing social reasons for their concern. Since World War II, it has become increasingly common for wives as well as husbands to work outside the home. The result has been a rapid growth in the need for comprehensive-care services for children under the age of seven — when formal schooling begins in all Nordic countries. The Finns have responded by establishing more than 1,700 state-subsidized day-care centers. There are also play groups run by local authorities, churches and other organizations, and playgrounds where children can be left under the supervision of "park nannies." These facilities are supplemented by state-approved child-care workers, who may take up to four children into their own homes for the day.

Demand for facilities continues to outrun supply throughout Scandinavia, however. In Sweden, for example, where some 80 percent of mothers with preschool children are part- or full-time workers, there was room in 1985 to accommodate only a third of the children in state-run day-care nurseries.

A plaster troll *(left)* — the shaggy giant of Scandinavian legend — towers over children playing on slides in an amusement park near the Norwegian town of Lillehammer. Elsewhere in the park *(above)*, a boy almost submerged in a tank of plastic balls prepares to toss one to a friend.

A park nanny watches over young children left to play in a Helsinki sandbox. Such private baby-sitters are often hired by working parents of preschoolers; but Finland also has some 1,600 outdoor playgrounds supervised by state employees, primarily for school-age children.

At lunch in a Helsinki kindergarten, five- and six-year-olds patiently wait their turn while two boys choose from a plate of open-faced sandwiches offered by a teacher. Some 290,000 Finnish children — more than half the children under school age — attend some kind of day-care facility.

In the reading room of Stockholm's multi-use House of Culture, youngsters wearing headphones listen attentively to children's records. The six-story complex was completed in 1974 and now attracts some 2.5 million visitors every year.

Imaginatively designed play areas are a feature of many urban centers in Scandinavia. Tapiola in Finland *(below)* provides brightly colored horses and a slide to entertain young children, while the Norwegian port of Bergen *(bottom)* recalls its seafaring traditions with a landlocked model boat.

5

In a tranquil corner of Helsinki's Sibe-
lius Park, a woman basks in the
summer sun beneath a statue by the
Finnish sculptor Aarre Aaltonen.
The work represents an episode from
Finland's national epic, the *Kalevala*.

THE QUEST FOR UTOPIA

In 1984, Scandinavia received an extraordinary compliment. A university professor in the United States published the results of a nine-year investigation into the social progress made by 107 countries with populations of at least one million. Denmark achieved first place in his world order of merit. Norway came second. Sweden was in fifth place, behind Austria and the Netherlands. Finland shared 10th place with West Germany. In contrast, France was 16th, Britain 25th, the United States 42nd, the Soviet Union 44th and Ethiopia last.

Richard Estes of the University of Pennsylvania School of Social Work based his statistical analysis on an index of 44 factors, including health, literacy, welfare programs, political stability, natural disasters, cultural diversity and the status of women. Only four of the factors were economic indicators. The study, he stressed, was not addressing the highly subjective questions of personal happiness and satisfaction with life. But it was designed to establish the general — rather than just the material — well-being of different nations.

Such an analysis inevitably invites controversy. Not even all Scandinavians were entirely satisfied with the findings; Estes received letters from Swedes who could not comprehend how Denmark had achieved a higher rating than their own country. Yet even with all allowances made, the Scandinavians' performance was remarkable. Indeed, the Nordic countries would have achieved 5 out of the top 10 places if Iceland had not been disqualified because of its small population. Certainly the island would have rated high in terms of health. The average life expectancy for Icelanders — 73.9 years for men and 79.4 for women — is the second highest in the world, after the Japanese, closely followed by that of the Swedes and the Norwegians.

Could it be, then, that Scandinavia is leading the rest of the world in the quest for the ideal society? Sociologists have been pondering that question for more than half a century — ever since 1936, when Sweden's social progress was held up for the world to see in Marquis Childs' renowned book, *Sweden: The Middle Way*. The Swedes, this American journalist claimed, had discovered a happy mean between the extremes of laissez-faire capitalism and totalitarian Communism. They were solving their problems in a sensible, pragmatic way at a time when other Western democracies were floundering and war clouds were gathering menacingly over Central Europe. "The struggle between the regressive forces of an outworn individualism and the new collective order has been overwhelming," Childs wrote. "If anywhere in modern life a balance has been struck, it seems to me to have been in the Scandinavian peninsula, and particularly in Sweden."

Childs was not suggesting that he had discovered Utopia "or even an approximation of Utopia"; and the Scandinavians themselves did not claim to have created some kind of paradise on earth. Nevertheless, the Nordic experiment continues to be a fashionable subject for both foreign journalists and sociologists to study and analyze. To what extent the Scandinavian approach to social problems has succeeded remains debatable. But two facts are beyond dispute; no other countries have been so adventurous and altruistic in introducing new social programs, and no others have acted for so long as a kind of social laboratory, producing innovations that other countries have sometimes greeted with incredulity, then found themselves imitating.

A popular tale from ancient Scandinavian history recounts how a scouting party from a small Viking fleet once traveled up the Seine. As the vessel approached a bend in the river beyond Rouen, a messenger from the Frankish overlord was sent out to discover the identity of the commander of the Viking fleet. Hailing the ship, the messenger called out: "What is the name of your captain?"

"There is no captain here. On this ship all are equals," came the reply.

The story, though surely apocryphal, does have some basis in fact. The Vikings held foreigners in slavery and acquired a reputation for appalling savagery in the lands they invaded. But among themselves, they achieved a relatively advanced social order and a greater degree of equality than other peoples of their time. Viking men could have freehold rights to land without paying dues or levies to an overlord. Women could own land and manage property (a ring of keys hanging from the waist symbolized their authority),

5

and divorce could be obtained easily and without shame.

One thousand years later, their descendants, using the mechanisms of modern bureaucratic states, set out to fulfill the Nordic yearning for equality by redistributing wealth through taxation and social benefits. Between 1891 and 1892, Denmark became the first European country to introduce health-insurance laws and old-age pensions on a contributory basis. These measures marked the beginning in Scandinavia of the most extensive social security systems in the world — systems now providing free health care and free education for all, paternity as well as maternity benefits, family allowances, pensions automatically adjusted to the cost of living, subsidized aids for the handicapped, homes for the aged, home assistance for families in need, shelters for battered wives, nurseries for the children of working parents.

Today's Vikings, however, have gone far beyond basic welfare legislation in striving to create a well-ordered, egalitarian society. They have sought to eliminate inequities caused by geography by providing services and communications, at enormous cost, to the many small communities isolated on islands, in mountain villages and in the far north. They have introduced the "social wage": a minimum income guaranteed by the state. (If a citizen earns less than this sum, the balance is made up by the local authorities.) They have been responsible for pioneering such innovations as antismoking campaigns, the compulsory wearing of seat belts in cars and compulsory sex education in schools.

They have also led the way in their approach to crime and punishment. Finland, for example, has not used the

death penalty for more than 150 years. In 1933, Denmark abolished corporal punishment as well as capital punishment. Later, radical penal reforms in Sweden included granting some prisoners the right to work at wages keyed to those paid on the outside, and the setting up of coeducational delinquent centers in which young miscreants of opposite sexes were permitted to cohabit. In 1973, Norway was the first country to make it illegal to strike a child, and in 1981, the Norwegian government was the first to appoint an ombudsman solely responsible for dealing with children's complaints of injustice.

The appointment of ombudsmen — independent investigators of public grievances — is one of the most widely imitated Scandinavian innovations. Since the 1960s, it has given a new word

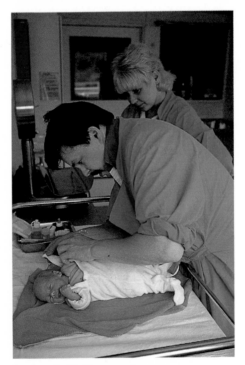

In a hospital in Espoo, a city near Helsinki, a father swaddles his newborn child while his wife looks on. The city's advanced health-care facilities provide parenting courses that prepare men to share the responsibilities of postnatal care.

to many languages and provided millions of people with means of appealing against unjust or arbitrary bureaucracy. The position originated in Sweden in 1809, when the duties of the official — properly known as the *justitieombudsman* and commonly called the "JO" — were expressly to see that judges and other public officials acted fairly and impartially. The case load has become so great that it has been split between four officers since 1976. In addition, Sweden has four supplementary offices of appeal, covering business and trade, consumer protection, the press and equal opportunity.

The Swedish ombudsmen receive thousands of written submissions a year (a letter need only be addressed "JO Stockholm" to be safely delivered), and every complaint, however trivial, must be investigated. Among the most difficult to assess are the many received from patients in mental hospitals. But even in these cases, the JO may be able to right injustices. In the 1960s, then-JO Alfred Bexelius told an interviewer about a complaint he had received from an alcoholic wife beater who had been confined to a mental institution for eight months because the examining doctor considered alcoholism to be a mental disease. A prison sentence for wife beating would have been shorter. Bexelius commented, "I personally don't like this man, but I will ask the government to compensate him for the extra time he was confined. It's important that society admits a fault."

Scandinavia has also been a world leader in the pursuit of equal rights for women. In 1906, Finland was the second country in the world — after New Zealand — to grant women electoral equality with men. In 1947, Denmark was the first Christian country to allow

women to be ordained as priests in its state church, thus setting an example that has been followed by all the Nordic countries except Finland. Later, Sweden encouraged female employment by offering wage subsidies to companies in which women employees made up 40 percent or more of the total staff.

Scandinavian women have been conspicuously successful in the political arena. In 1980, Iceland had the world's first popularly elected woman head of state. The new president, Vigdis Finnbogadottir, had earlier set another major precedent — as one of the first single women in Iceland to win the legal right to adopt a child.

By the mid-1980s, the proportion of women in various Nordic parliaments was 31 percent for Finland, 28 percent for Sweden, 24 percent for Denmark and 15 percent for Iceland. Most striking was Norway, where 34 percent of the Storting's 157 seats in 1986 were held by women. Norwegian Prime Minister Gro Harlem Brundtland's Labor party was instrumental in achieving equality, adopting a rule that 40 percent of its candidates for public office be women. When Brundtland ran for prime minister a second time in 1985, she had little difficulty finding qualified women to fill Cabinet posts. In 1986, eight out of 18 Cabinet members were women, giving Norway the highest proportion of women in top-level government positions in the world.

While Scandinavian countries have continually sought new ways to improve the quality of life, they have also been alert to blocking external influences that might conceivably debase existing values. Of all the Nordic states, none has more sternly resisted the encroachments of the outside world than Iceland, a country that has had so little immigration that it can be said, without much exaggeration, that all of its inhabitants are distantly related. Here, tradition dies hard — a fact reflected by the centuries-old custom of assigning people's names. Icelandic women keep their maiden names after marriage. Children's surnames are composed of the possessive form of the father's Christian name suffixed by *son* (son) or *dottir* (daughter) as appropriate. Thus,

143

a husband might be named Njal Sigurdursson, his wife Vigdis Johnsdottir and their children Thor Njalsson and Bryndis Njalsdottir. It is a custom that can make for considerable confusion — if not awkward misunderstandings — when an Icelandic family registers at a hotel abroad. Furthermore, so many names are identical that the Icelandic telephone directory is arranged by first names and includes the profession of each subscriber to help identification.

In 1964, the British poet W. H. Auden wrote of Iceland:

Fortunate island
where all men are equal
but not vulgar — not yet.

The comment is still valid today. The spirit of egalitarianism is so genuine that only two people — the president and the island's Lutheran bishop — are addressed by their titles. Iceland remains a nation without a monarchy or an aristocracy of any kind; in essence, it is a classless society without divisions by wealth, education or background. As for vulgarity, it is still resisted by official measures that are designed to safeguard the purity of the ancient Icelandic language and to preserve the highest traditions of Icelandic culture.

For example, the 3,000-strong American NATO base at Keflavik is seen as a threat to Iceland's traditional way of life and is subject to strict controls. Uniforms are not allowed to be worn off base. An 11:30 p.m. to 6 a.m. curfew is in effect for the lower ranks. And the Americans' television station, transmitting 24 hours a day, was converted to cable transmission following Icelandic objections that it was "an unacceptable invasion of national life." By the same token, Icelandic television is restricted to about five hours of transmission every day except Tuesday,

which is set aside as a "family day" of complete rest. Until 1984, screens also remained blank during July — when most people take summer vacations.

In this way, Icelanders have avoided domination of their leisure hours by television, a medium that, in many countries, seems to have gained the importance of a life-support machine. Icelanders are able to devote more time to creative, cultural and sports activities. In particular, they maintain their reputation for being avid readers. "Better shoeless than bookless" goes an old proverb. On a per capita basis, Iceland probably has more bookstores than any other country in the world. Although there are only 250,000 inhabitants, about 40 new books are published every month. There are also art galleries, a national theater and an opera company — all heavily subsidized by the state. And the government further promotes culture by paying salaries to outstanding artists, writers and composers.

Among other Nordic nationals, the Norwegians are perhaps the most protective of their own culture and old values. When the people shocked their government in a 1972 referendum by voting against joining the EEC, one of the reasons for the referendum's outcome was a vague fear that EEC membership might somehow undermine the traditional way of life of Norway's close-knit agricultural and fishing communities. By the same token, not all Norwegians were overjoyed when the rising price of oil in the 1970s suggested the possibility that their country might soon achieve the world's highest standard of living. Instead, there were fears that the oil riches would upset society's framework by inflating the economy, destroying long-established, small-scale industries that would be un-

A "FREE CITY" IN THE HEART OF COPENHAGEN

In 1971, when the Danish army moved out of quarters in the Christianshavn district of Copenhagen, their old barracks were gradually occupied by squatters who renamed the area the Free City of Christiania. In the abandoned military compound, the squatters established a largely self-sufficient community with a bohemian lifestyle, attracting artists and artisans as well as drifters.

As the fame of Christiania spread, its floating population swelled to about 1,000, including many short-term foreign visitors. Since 1972, it has gained a degree of official recognition by paying token rent to the Ministry of Defense. But its existence remains highly controversial. Swedish and Norwegian authorities as well as Danes have claimed that Christiania is the primary Nordic connection for hashish and other drugs, and demands to close it down have frequently been made at Nordic Council meetings.

Residents relax by a half-built mill.

An elaborate mural incorporating Buddhist and North American Indian motifs covers a wall in Christiania.

A painted sign indicates the colony entrance.

A girl, one of some 200 children in Christiania, plays outside the wooden hut where she lives.

During a race for handicapped athletes in Oslo's Bislet Stadium, a blind runner *(right foreground)* is guided with a rope by a sighted companion. It is Norway's policy to mainstream the disabled as much as possible, and special events for the handicapped are held at many major track and field events.

able to compete for skilled labor, and debasing the simple, nonmaterialistic virtues of rural life.

Many Norwegians argued that the new riches from "black gold" should be used to improve the quality of life, to keep unemployment down and to help Third World countries, rather than to finance flashy development projects and create a wealthy elite. The new-found revenue from oil and natural gas allowed generous government support for flagging industries and unlimited investment in new ones. As a result, the unemployment rate in Norway in the mid-1980s was among the lowest in Europe, and many of the small, uneconomic communities were saved from extinction by heavy subsidization.

The other Nordic countries have been less conservative than Norway and Iceland in seeking to preserve traditional ways and values; all, however, have been extremely active in striving to protect their natural environment. Scandinavians have become especially anxious about the development of nuclear power. Only Sweden and Finland have built nuclear reactors, and Sweden is now committed to closing down its plants by the year 2010. This represents an enormous sacrifice on the part of a country that has virtually no coal or oil resources but, ironically, has the largest uranium deposits in Europe. A few years ago, a parliamentary committee estimated that the cost to Sweden of phasing out nuclear power would range from 5 to 10 billion kronor ($580 million to $1.2 billion) annually for each year the reactors could have been used after the cutoff date.

Opposition to the production of nuclear weapons has been equally strong. The Scandinavians are technically capable of developing these tools of mass destruction, but all five countries have signed and ratified the 1963 Test Ban Treaty and the Nonproliferation Treaty; the latter was agreed upon in 1968 by Britain, the Soviet Union and the United States to contain the spread of nuclear weapons. Finland hosted the first East-West Strategic Arms Limitation Talks in 1970 and has championed a proposal for creating a nuclear-free zone in Scandinavia. Denmark and Norway, though members of NATO, have refused to have nuclear weapons deployed on their soil in peacetime. Sweden, despite the fact that it is extremely defense conscious (it has one of the most powerful air forces in the world), has formally and unilaterally renounced all nuclear, chemical and biological weapons.

Not content with trying to protect their own environment and promote social well-being at home, the Scandi-navians have also consistently concerned themselves with the welfare of the world at large. They have devoted large sums of money for aid to under-developed countries, and they have provided troops for many of the United Nations' peace-keeping operations. Right or wrong, some Nordic countries have been outspoken on major world foreign-policy issues. Sweden's forth-right condemnation of the United States' participation in the Vietnam War attracted hundreds of American deserters and draft-evaders to its shores. And Denmark, ever vigilant in the cause of human rights, now operates a rehabilitation and research center for torture victims that has helped people from countries as far apart as Argentina and Afghanistan.

Furthermore, no other group of countries has produced so many people of stature to serve as international

Children practice their double-handed backhands at the Royal Tennis Club in Stockholm. Since Björn Borg's success in the 1970s, Sweden's unrivaled facilities, including 1,400 indoor courts, have made it the strongest tennis nation, per capita, in the world.

146

peacemakers and mediators. One such was the celebrated Norwegian explorer Fridtjof Nansen, who led his country's delegation to the first assembly of the League of Nations in 1920 and subsequently won worldwide renown as a humanitarian and diplomat. He particularly involved himself in famine relief and the repatriation of prisoners of war, and was responsible for the introduction of the "Nansen Passport," an internationally accepted identity card for stateless and displaced persons.

Among the many Scandinavians who followed Nansen's example was Count Folke Bernadotte, a nephew of King Gustavus V of Sweden. As leader of the Swedish Red Cross, he arranged the exchange of thousands of World War II prisoners; he was assassinated in 1948, while attempting, on behalf of the United Nations, to mediate between Jews and Arabs in Palestine. Two of his contemporaries were Norway's Trygve Lie, first secretary general of the United Nations, and Raoul Wallenberg, the Swedish diplomat who saved the lives of an estimated 100,000 Jews in Nazi-occupied Budapest, and who disappeared mysteriously after being taken

into custody by Soviet troops in January of 1945. Another possibly martyred Swede was Dag Hammarskjöld, also a United Nations secretary general, who was killed in an air crash in 1961 while on a peace mission to the Congo.

Scandinavians, then, have much to be proud of. In 1965, a newspaper article by Danish writer Henrik Stangerup reflected the optimism of a great many people at that time:

We are experiencing today in Scandinavia one of the most important experiments of world history. That may sound pretentious, yet it isn't. Scandinavia of today is the world's avant-garde society. What is taking place among us will happen in other countries tomorrow, as soon as they have reached a comparable level of freedom and welfare. We have an almost unlimited freedom of speech and freedom of the press. We have a standard of living that is the envy of the whole world. We simply have every imaginable opportunity to lead our lives in free development of our human and creative possibilities. . . . If we only know how to use our freedom and to realize it in our lives, our experience . . . will be of profit to the entire world around us.

Scandinavian self-esteem was then probably at its highest — and justifiably so. The social progress of the Nordic countries had been truly remarkable and was much envied by most foreign observers. But the enthusiasm was already by no means universal. From the mid-1950s onward, in some Western countries, there had been a growing volume of adverse comment on the world's most advanced welfare states.

Such sniping was encouraged in 1959 when U.S. President Dwight D. Eisenhower publicly referred to an unnamed Scandinavian country that was engaged, he said, in an "experiment in almost complete paternalism," a form of total welfare that, he claimed, had undermined the moral fiber of the whole nation and resulted in large-scale drunkenness and suicide. His speech was bitterly condemned all over Scandinavia; later, on a visit to Sweden, the president, admitting that he had been mistaken, publicly apologized. But seeds of doubt had been sown, and thereafter, some members of the foreign press focused less on Scandinavian enlightenment and more on what they considered to be signs of moral decline.

COLLECTIVE LIVING IN A DANISH COMMUNE

In 1978, eighty-five Danes seeking a viable alternative lifestyle pooled their resources to buy a 1,000-acre estate at Svanholm, 30 miles west of Copenhagen. They dedicated their new community to the principles of collective decision-making, equal job responsibility between the sexes and ecological food production. Today, Svanholm has about 100 adult members, plus about 80 children, making it the largest commune in Denmark.

The residents live in small groups — from five to 20 adults — in dwellings scattered across the estate. Meals are communal and are served in the single, large kitchen; children are taken care of in a day nursery while their parents are at work.

Only one third of the adults have jobs outside the commune; the rest work on the estate in a wide range of occupations: growing crops; managing the forest and garden; raising farm animals, rabbits and honey bees; producing pinewood furniture from the commune factory and tools from the forge. Mechanically minded residents service the jointly owned cars; others maintain the buildings. Creative skills, too, are put to use in workshops, turning out candles, ceramics and leather goods.

In keeping with the prevailing collectivist philosophy, all income from the sale of produce and services is pooled. From this fund, expenses are paid, including mortgage debts, investments, union dues, doctors' bills and small personal allowances for each resident.

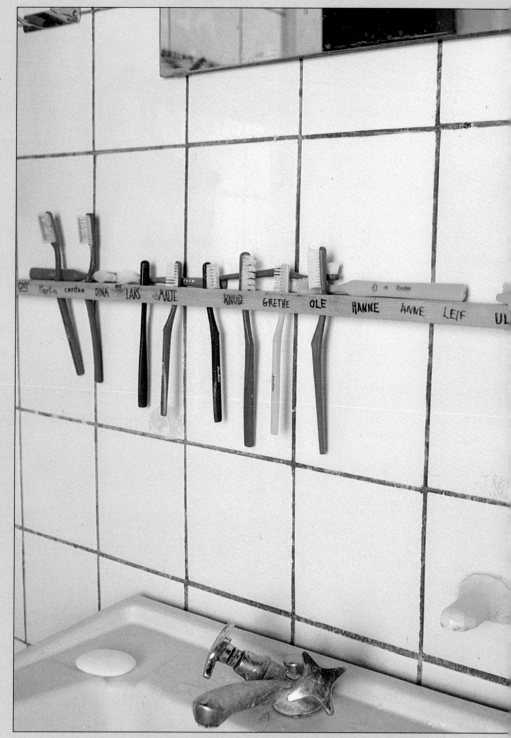

In a commune bathroom, a toothbrush holder bears the names of more than a dozen residents.

In the sewing room, two women patch garments with scraps of material. Residents leave clothes they no longer want on the shelves for other members to wear or to use for mending.

A woman takes her turn on duty in the cafeteria, which can accommodate about 200 people at one sitting. Hot and cold selections are available at both midday and evening meals.

5

To a degree, the Scandinavians — or more precisely, the daringly progressive Swedes and Danes — invited sensational publicity abroad by their far-ranging efforts to free sexuality from the fears and repressions of the past. During the 1960s, when the advent of the contraceptive pill heralded the dawn of a new permissive age, Sweden set the pace by reducing taboos on sex before marriage and making public-school sex education compulsory for children aged 12 and older. More controversially, Denmark was, in 1970, the first country to legalize pornography. Sweden soon followed Denmark in abolishing censorship, and tourists flocked to Copenhagen and Stockholm to take advantage of live sex shows, porn shops, houses of prostitution disguised as massage parlors, and movie theaters and bookstores offering fare unobtainable in other countries.

By the mid-1970s, it was clear that such measures were a mixed blessing. Contrary to expectation, sex crimes increased; prostitution flourished; and the Copenhagen porn trade became a center for gangsters, pimps, drug pushers and petty criminals. The result was a backlash against the extremes of the permissive age that led to the banning in Denmark and Sweden of live sex shows and child pornography.

Far more ominous for the well-being of society than the excesses of permissiveness, however, were the events that followed the world oil crisis of 1973. Alone of the Scandinavian nations, Norway was eventually able to benefit — as a producer in the North Sea fields — from the dramatic rise in energy prices that the oil crisis triggered. Elsewhere, the great Nordic experiment was suddenly subjected to the harsh test of economic duress, and serious weaknesses began to show. Strikes were more frequent; welfare fraud and tax evasion became commonplace; and the Scandinavians themselves began to question the wisdom of trying to maintain costly social programs.

The new concerns manifested themselves in different ways in the different countries. In Denmark, a tax lawyer named Mogens Glistrup unexpectedly became a folk hero. He had defiantly proclaimed on television that he had a personal income of five million kroner (about $700,000 at the time) and yet, through a clever manipulation of the nation's tax laws, he had made no contribution at all to the national revenues. Glistrup won the admiration of hundreds of thousands of Danes, who shared his opinion that enterprise was being stifled by the demands of a voracious welfare state.

Glistrup formed a political party whose main objectives were the reduction of income tax and a massive cutback in welfare spending. In 1973, his Progress party won 28 seats, making it the second-largest group in the Folketing (Parliament). This ground was largely lost in the 1981 elections; by then, the charismatic Glistrup was involved in a complicated law suit that led to his expulsion from Parliament and a three-year jail sentence for tax fraud. Nevertheless, his few years of glory were generally regarded as evidence that a large proportion of the Danish people felt that the welfare system had become too expensive and that there was too much bureaucracy and government interference.

In the meantime, Swedish passions had been stirred by an equally well-publicized case. In January of 1976,

A Turkish woman *(above)* shops at an open-air market in the Stockholm suburb of Rinkeby, while nearby, immigrant children *(right)* gather at an outdoor café. Of Sweden's 8.3 million people 1 in 8 is either foreign-born or first-generation Swedish.

a rehearsal of Strindberg's *Dance of Death* at the Royal Dramatic Theater in Stockholm ended abruptly when police arrived and ordered its director, the celebrated movie maker Ingmar Bergman, to accompany them immediately to a tax court inquiry. At the same time, the tax authorities searched Bergman's house, as well as his lawyer's house, and confiscated various documents. The following month, Bergman was charged with tax evasion and "careless income tax returns."

The Bergman case became the subject of heated debate in print, on the radio and on television, especially after an official investigation had cleared Bergman of wrongdoing and led to his receiving a large tax refund from the authorities. Then-Prime Minister Olof Palme talked to Bergman on the telephone to express his regrets at the clumsy way the case had been handled. But Bergman was not easily mollified. After spending some time in the hospital to recover from what he described as "nearly unbearable humiliation," he announced that he was leaving Sweden to work abroad. Before his departure, Bergman savagely attacked what he called the "ideology of gray compromise" of the Social Democrats, who proclaimed the virtue of costly social reform while they ignored the destructive effects of a bureaucracy that was spreading "like a fast-growing cancer."

The cause célèbre came as a grim reminder of the intrusive power of Sweden's highly regimented bureaucracy. Income tax agents have the power to enter the offices of taxpayers without warning and have the right to search private homes once they have obtained a court order. They may also obtain details of private accounts from banks. But the controversy surrounding the Bergman case spotlighted an equally significant fact: that the public at large was automatically sympathetic to anyone who was in conflict with the tax authorities. Deep down, many respectable citizens considered that tax evasion was not a crime but a natural response to unreasonable demands by the state.

Soon after the Bergman trial, the high rate of taxation again came under public attack when Astrid Lindgren, author of best-selling children's stories, was advised that she had to pay the tax board 102 percent of her 1976 income. This absurdity was the result of bad arithmetic and an anomaly in the way that taxes were charged. The author replied by contributing to the newspaper *Expressen* a charming story about a never-never land where logic could be manipulated to enable people to take as many deductions as they wanted.

More sensationally still, in 1983, Ove Rainer, Sweden's minister of the judiciary, was accused by a newspaper of paying minuscule tax on a personal income of more than two million kronor ($270,000). Like thousands of other citizens, Ranier had acted well within the law when he exploited a loophole in the tax regulations. In this case, however, Rainer was forced to resign from his government position because, morally, he had become an embarrassment to the Social Democrats.

By that point, people in all the five Nordic countries were feeling heavily burdened by taxation. Throughout Scandinavia, the response was a steady growth of the so-called underground, or barter, economy: A Norwegian accountant trades his services to a client in exchange for having his cabin cruiser painted; a Finnish builder repairs a

5

lawyer's roof in exchange for free advice; a Swedish doctor gives an auto mechanic a consultation in exchange for having his car serviced. Similarly, in Iceland and Denmark during the early 1980s, it was difficult to get private work done without resorting to paying for services in unrecorded cash.

High welfare costs were beginning to weaken the entire Nordic economy. In Sweden, for example, employment was affected as social insurance payments for staff became an intolerable burden for many small businesses. Restaurants, hotels and building firms cut their salaried labor force to an absolute minimum, preferring to subcontract work where possible. Small stores asked customers whether they wanted a receipt or not; if the answer was no, the shopkeeper could illegally save on sales tax payments. Generous sick pay almost equal to normal wages was a disincentive to labor. A study by the Employers' Federation revealed that Sweden's industrial workers had the highest rate of sick leave in the world, and that fully 10 percent of the work force was continually absent.

Gunnar Myrdal, 1974 Nobel Prize winner in economics, claimed that the tax system was "turning Swedes into a gang of hustlers" and "making 9 out of 10 Swedes criminals." Quite simply, it appeared that the idealism and public spiritedness that had built up the Scandinavian welfare society had begun to give way to rampant self-centeredness and self-interest.

"The core of the crisis," wrote Bent Rold Andersen, a former Danish minister of social affairs, "is that the ordinary citizen not only openly and without compunction takes part in the underground economy and exploits the system of public services, but also hails others who do, and sees any attempts by the authorities to restrain this tendency as an infringement of his rights."

In 1984, novelist Per Olov Enquist summed up his country's dilemma:

In Sweden they dreamt of being able to produce the good human being by legislation; or more precisely, of legislating evil out of existence. It was no bad dream created by wicked people. It developed out of a Christian, a Lutheran, sense of responsibility: "Am I not my brother's keeper?" The problem arose when the sense of responsibility for one's neighbor drove the society to take too much responsibility away from him: He then lacked responsibility, and the society acquired the power.

Enquist might have been describing the experience of Scandinavia as a whole. To varying degrees, all of the Nordic countries had striven, by way of legislation, to create a more just and humane society. But they never had a sure formula to follow. In drawing up a balance sheet of their successes and failures, it is important to avoid the temptation of overemphasizing the inevitable mistakes. The Scandinavians are so self-critical and analytical that it is easy for outsiders to catalogue the many shortcomings in their welfare states. The Nordic countries provide an abundance of statistics that chart increases in crime, alcoholism, drug use, divorce and suicide. The fact that many other Western countries have experienced far greater increases is not seen by them as a redeeming factor. They set their own high standards of acceptable behavior and here lies another Nordic paradox: While the Scandinavians have a reputation for being extraordinarily permissive in matters pertaining to sexual liberation, they are, in other ways, restrictive and somewhat puritan.

Alcohol, for example, has long been regarded as the great enemy of the people. Between 1917 and 1955, Swedes could buy liquor only if they had ration books, and these were not granted to married women, citizens under 25 years old or known alcoholics. In the 1920s, Finland introduced total prohibition with disastrous results; as in the United States, consumption multiplied and illegal production and bootlegging boomed. Now the war on the "evil spirits" is waged by way of extremely high prices and rigid licensing hours in all the Scandinavian countries except Denmark. Drink is distributed through state monopolies and drunk driving is severely punished. Convicted drivers may find themselves serving on a road gang. In one celebrated case, a Finnish Cabinet minister — the law is the same for all — was sentenced to a period of labor on the site of Helsinki Airport.

Despite the heavy penalties exacted, alcoholism is currently regarded as a greater problem than ever. Swedes point out that their alcohol consumption per capita is less than half that of the French, Spanish, Italians or West Germans, but nonetheless, the state authorities are deeply concerned. The indications, they say, are that people are starting to drink alcohol at a younger age, and drunk driving still accounts for one third of all traffic accidents. Swedish sociologists have also detected a close link between the rising crime figures and the increase in alcohol and drug consumption.

By their own high standards, the Nordic countries have also fallen short in their bid to achieve true egalitarianism. Many inequalities still exist. For example, a university education is free to all who pass their secondary-school examinations, but support grants are inadequate, and so the system inevitably favors candidates from wealthier families. Then again, legislation on equal rights for women has failed to eliminate sex discrimination. On the average, women in all five countries are paid less than their male counterparts. In Finland, women are technically more advanced than elsewhere, and 40 percent of the lawyers and 20 percent of the judges are women. But working-class and rural communities are still patriarchal. Few men help with domestic chores, but women tend to do more of the heavy industrial jobs, such as crane operator and welder, giving force to the old Finnish proverb: "The man steers the boat while the woman rows."

In the mid-1980s, the rate of female employment was among the highest in the Western world. The figures ranged from a high of 47 percent in Sweden to a low of 40 percent in Norway, as compared with an average of 30 percent for other countries. However, the record was not quite as impressive as it appeared, since a substantial proportion of employed women were, in fact, working only part time. Furthermore, many women were handicapped by insufficient child-care facilities.

Perhaps the deepest criticism made of the Nordic-style welfare state is that it encroaches too much on the private life of the citizen. Sweden, in particular, has been charged on this count. Critics point to the police's use of television cameras to scan public places for drunks and drug dealers; the existence of highly developed computerized systems that keep a detailed record of every citizen's progress and circumstances, including information about health, education, tax and insurance situation, credit worthiness and any traffic violations; and the increasing

An armed policewoman talks to a colleague while on duty outside the royal palace in Stockholm. All Swedish police — including women officers, who account for about 10 percent of the uniformed force — are equipped with .765-caliber Walter revolvers.

frequency with which children under the age of 15 who are believed to be victims of physical, sexual or psychological abuse are separated from their parents by the state.

In 1983, there was a major public controversy over the number of children — roughly 1 in 1,000 each year — who were being taken into custodial care against their parents' wishes. The authorities called an international press conference to answer criticisms, but they only heightened misgivings when they explained that the practice was a result of the increasing psychological pressure on Swedish family life. In the light of the wide and hostile foreign publicity given to this issue, Arne Ruth, editor-in-chief of Sweden's largest daily newspaper, *Dagens Nyheter,* wrote: "Sweden has definitely fallen from grace. If the cliché of political journalism in Western Europe 15 years ago was of Sweden as the realized utopia of industrial peace and social justice, the stereotype of the Eighties appears to be of Sweden as the home of Big Brother."

This view is blatantly unfair. If Arne Ruth's claim were true, the state would hardly choose to discuss its problems so openly, nor would so many citizens so flagrantly defy certain aspects of the law if they felt there was a "Big Brother." Yet even friends of Scandinavia might agree that there is far too much bureaucracy and state control. As Bent Rold Andersen has asked: "Is it good for human beings to be cosseted, to live in a welfare state, protected not only against external risks, but also against the consequences of their own mistakes, incompetence, or even laziness, and to be deprived of the fruits, not only of luck, but also of their own efforts? No one really knows."

Certainly, the Nordic countries still

have many serious socioeconomic problems to resolve, and others lie ahead. For example, birth rates in Nordic countries are among the lowest in the world. Will there be enough people of working age to finance the pensions and medical care of the postwar "baby-boom" generation when they reach old age? Will it be possible, in times of rising expectations and expenses, to maintain far-ranging social security systems without imposing levels of taxation that discourage enterprise?

Such problems lie in the future. Meanwhile, the Scandinavian social experiment has proved surprisingly resilient in the face of rapidly changing economic conditions. Significantly, for all the many criticisms of the Nordic-style welfare state, not even the most vociferous antitax groups have ever proposed abandoning the system; and though they may differ in their plans for modifications, all the major political parties are unanimous in their wish to safeguard their version of the existing system. "What really matters," says Bent Rold Andersen, "is whether we have succeeded in abolishing poverty and illiteracy, in reducing tensions between social classes, in promoting social mobility, and in dignifying the common man so that he feels on an equal footing with the rich and the famous."

By those criteria, the Scandinavian experiment must be judged a success — albeit not an unqualified one. After more than half a century, Marquis Childs' concluding judgment of "the middle way" is still as valid as ever: "Whatever the future may bring there will remain the record of a people who cultivated their garden, their rocky, remote, lonely garden with patience, with courage, and with an extraordinary degree of intelligence." □

Jagged cliffs and glacier-bearing mountains tower above the still waters of the Nord Fjord near Loen in western Norway. Such forbidding and majestic landscapes have remained virtually unchanged since the days of the Vikings a millennium ago.

ACKNOWLEDGMENTS

The index for this book was prepared by Vicki Robinson. For their help in the preparation of this volume, the editors also express their gratitude to the following people and institutions: Carolyn Alcock, London; Nils-Göran Andersson, Wärtsilä Arctic Design and Marketing, Helsinki; Judy Aspinall, London; Kerstin Asp-Johnsson, Cultural Attaché, Swedish Embassy, London; Brit Bartz-Johannessen, West Norway Tourist Board, Bergen; Ola Hiis Bergh, Bergen Tourist Board, Norway; Kaj Björkman, Stockholm; Martin D. Blake, Press Office, ASEA, Sweden; Mike Brown, London; Walter Collins, Oscar Woollens, London; Danish Embassy, London; Sigvard Estvall, ASEA, Sweden; Annelise Fibaek, Copenhagen; Finnish Embassy, London; Finnish Tourist Board, London; Tryggve Fitje, West Norway Tourist Board, Bergen; Karin Fredgård, Stockholm; Christina Guggenberger, Stockholm Information Service; Eva Gustavsson, Swedish Tourist Board, Stockholm; Liz Hodgson, London; Matti Kohva, Finnfacts, Helsinki; Martin Leighton, Hove, England; Jens and Inger Lindgren, Stockholm; Doris Løkke, Norwegian Tourist Office, Paris; Monika Lubkowska, Jonas Company, London; Ulla Nicolai, Christiania, Copenhagen; Kurt Nielsen, Danish Tourist Board, Copenhagen; Gunnar Nørstad, Press Department, Carlsberg, Copenhagen; Norwegian Embassy, London; Orheim family, Mundal Hotel, Fjaerland, Norway; Captain Jaako Pohjola, Board of Navigation, Helsinki; Paul Reeves, Scott Howard Associates Ltd., London; Karl Skarheim, Norwegian Tourist Board, Oslo; Leif Sundman, Finnfacts, Helsinki; Swedish Embassy, London; Deborah Thompson, London; Ari Valjakka, Personnel and Communications, Wärtsilä, Helsinki; Benny Villumsen, Tulip, Vejle, Denmark.

BIBLIOGRAPHY

BOOKS

Allen, Hilary, *Norway and Europe in the 1970s.* Norway: Universitetsforlaget, 1979.

Bacon, Walter, *Finland.* London: Robert Hale and Company, 1970.

Baedeker's Scandinavia. London: The Automobile Association, 1982.

Blunt, Wilfred, *The Compleat Naturalist: A Life of Linnaeus.* London: William Collins, 1971.

Bredsdorff, Elias, *Hans Christian Andersen.* London: Phaidon Press, 1975.

Brown, Dale, *The Cooking of Scandinavia.* New York: Time-Life Books, 1968.

Childs, Marquis:
The Middle Way on Trial. New Haven, Connecticut: Yale University Press, 1980.
Sweden: The Middle Way. London: Faber and Faber, 1936.

Connery, Donald S., *The Scandinavians.* London: Eyre and Spottiswoode, 1966.

Derry, Thomas, *A History of Scandinavia.* London: George Allen and Unwin, 1970.

Elstob, Eric C., *Sweden: A Traveller's History.* Suffolk, England: Boydell Press, 1979.

Engle, Eloise, and Lauri Paananen, *The Winter War.* London: Sidgwick and Jackson, 1973.

Estes, Richard J., *The Social Progress of Nations.* New York: Praeger Publishers, 1984.

Fullerton, Brian, and Alan F. Williams, *Scandinavia.* London: Chatto and Windus, 1972.

Graham-Campbell, James, *The Viking World.* London: Frances Lincoln Publishers, 1980.

Graham-Campbell, James, and Dafydd Kidd, *The Vikings.* London: British Museum Publications, 1980.

Greve, Tim, *Haakon VII of Norway.* London: C. Hurst and Company, 1983.

Handbook of Denmark. Copenhagen: Danish Foreign Ministry, 1974.

Harrison-Church, R. J., ed., *North-Western Europe.* Bucks, England: Hulton, 1980.

Huntford, Roland, *The New Totalitarians.* London: Allen Lane, 1971.

John, Brian S., *Scandinavia: A New Geography.* London: Longman Group, 1984.

Jones, Mervyn, *The Sami of Lapland.* London: Minority Rights Group, 1982.

Jones, W. Glyn, *Denmark.* London: Ernest Benn, 1970.

Klinge, Matti, *A Brief History of Finland.* Finland: Otava Publishing Company, 1981.

Lauring, Palle, *A History of the Kingdom of Denmark.* Copenhagen: Host and Sons Forlag, 1960.

Lucas, E. L., *Ibsen and Strindberg.* London: Cassell, 1962.

Magnusson, Magnus, *Vikings!* London: The Bodley Head, 1980.

Magnusson, Sigurdur A., *Northern Sphinx: Iceland and the Icelanders from the Settlement to the Present.* London: C. Hurst and Company, 1977.

Maze, Edward, *Creative Sweden.* Stockholm: Gebers Forlag, 1965.

Mead, W. R.:
Finland. London: Ernest Benn, 1968.
An Historical Geography of Scandinavia. London: Academic Press, 1981.
The Scandinavian Northlands. Oxford, England: Oxford University Press, 1974.

Mead, W. R., and Wendy Hall, *Scandinavia.* London: Thames and Hudson, 1972.

Mead, W. R., and S. H. Jaatinen, *The Aland Islands.* Newton Abbot, England: David and Charles, 1975.

Mead, W. R., and Helmer Smeds, *Winter in Finland.* London: Hugh Evelyn, 1967.

Nordic Statistical Secretariat, *Yearbook of Nordic Statistics.* Stockholm: The Nordic Council, 1983.

Popperwell, Ronald G., *Norway.* London: Ernest Benn, 1972.

Richards, J. M., *A Guide to Finnish Architecture.* London: Hugh Evelyn, 1966.

Roberts, Michael, *Gustavus Adolphus and the Rise of Sweden.* London: The English Universities Press, 1973.

Sawyer, Peter H., *Kings and Vikings: Scandinavia and Europe AD 700-1100.* London: Methuen, 1982.

Scherman, Katharine, *Iceland: Daughter of Fire.* London: Victor Gollancz, 1976.

Scobbie, Irene, *Sweden.* London: Ernest Benn, 1972.

Selz, Jean, *Edvard Munch.* Paris: Flammarion, 1974.

Simpson, Colin, *The Viking Circle.* London: Hodder and Stoughton, 1967.

Simpson, Jacqueline, *Everyday Life in the Viking Age.* London: B. T. Batsford, 1967.

Sjøvold, Thorleif, *The Viking Ships in Oslo.* Oslo: Universitets Oldsaksamling, 1979.

Spencer, Arthur, *The Norwegians: How They Live and Work.* Newton Abbot, England: David and Charles, 1984.

Thomas, David, *Henrik Ibsen.* London: The Macmillan Press, 1983.

Tietze, Wolf, *Norway.* Berne, Switzerland: Kümmerly and Frey, 1980.

Turner, Barry, and Gunilla Nordquist, *The Other European Community.* London: Weidenfeld and Nicolson, 1982.

Wadensjö, Gösta, *Meet Sweden.* Malmö, Sweden: LiberHermods, 1979.

Wilson, David, ed., *The Northern World.* London: Thames and Hudson, 1980.

Wuorinen, John H., *A History of Finland.* New York: Columbia University Press, 1965.

PERIODICALS AND PAMPHLETS

"Basic Statistics of Iceland." Ministry for Foreign Affairs, Iceland.

"Factsheet Denmark." Press and Cultural Relations Department of the Ministry of Foreign Affairs, Denmark.

"Fact Sheets on Sweden." The Swedish Institute, Stockholm.

"Finland." *The Guardian*, November 6, 1984.

"Finland: A Reassessment." W. R. Mead, The Geographical Association, 1983.

"Finland: A Special Report." *The Times of Lon-*

don, November 14, l984.

"Finnish Features." Ministry of Foreign Affairs, Helsinki.

Iceland Review.

Look at Finland.

"The Nordic Enigma." *Daedalus: The Journal of the American Academy of Arts and Sciences,* Winter 1984.

"Nordic Voices." *Daedalus: The Journal of the American Academy of Arts and Sciences,* Spring 1984.

"Norway." *Financial Times* Survey, April 18, l984.

"Norway Information." The Royal Norwegian Ministry of Foreign Affairs, Norway.

Sweden Now.

PICTURE CREDITS

Credits from left to right are separated by semicolons, from top to bottom by dashes.

INDEX

Page numbers in italics refer to illustrations of the subject mentioned.

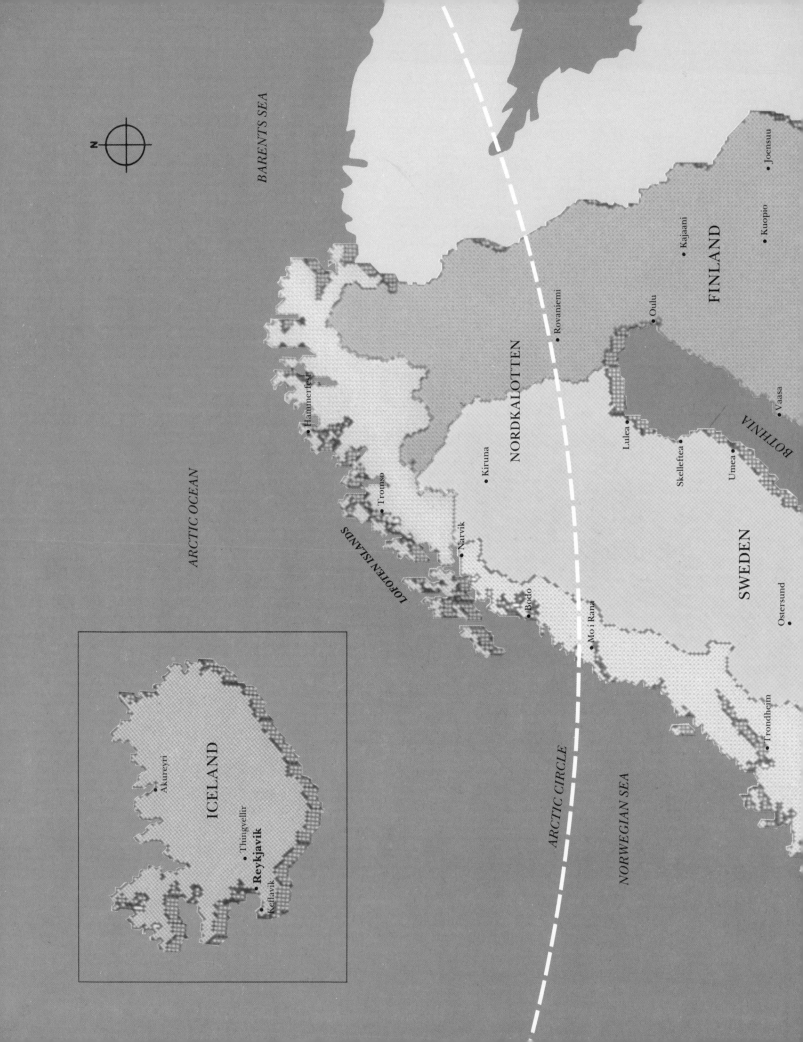